Along the tracks of Cobb and Co.

The Western Run

History speaking for itself ...

Research and compilation by Hazel Johnson

In memory of Kenneth Victor & Mavis Rosa Johnson, and all people past, who built this great country of Australia—sunburnt, vast, resilient and open-hearted.

Author's Note

"There was busy life on all the stages when they were kings of the road—wayside hotels, with refreshment places and mail-changes between, made welcome breaks along the tracks ... The swift, mechanical transport that took up the running did not need a halting place at every 30 miles or so ... once promising hamlets began to fade ...

The westerners felt they had lost something that was almost an Australian institution, a romantic and picturesque feature of their homeland that nothing could replace."

Courtesy of John Elliott, writer/photographer

I've always had a love for history. As an Australian, I find the story of Cobb and Co. a powerful reminder of our country's pioneering past. The people behind this great firm—and others who helped build modern Australia—have my admiration. Their grit, determination, and resilience come through clearly in the stories shared in this book.

What I've learned is simple: the people of the past weren't so different from us. They were bold entrepreneurs, imaginative minds, and practical problem-solvers. They faced the relentless rhythm of daily work—rain, hail, or shine—much like today's farmers, vegetable and fruit growers, and dairy producers. And they met challenges with humour too, as illustrated in this light-hearted anecdote:

"At an unnamed change station, the boss would flick off the covering of the food and say, What would you like—sheep, lamb, mutton, or ram?"

You may ask, What makes my books different? This series explores how Cobb and Co. and the postal service contributed to the building of the nation we know today. Instead of retelling history through a present-day lens, I've used original writings from the 1800s to the mid-1900s, letting history speak for itself.

These authentic excerpts transport readers to the box seat beside the driver, rattling along dusty coach tracks and stopping at bustling change stations. There's something powerful about hearing the words as they were first written—raw, honest, humorous, and true to their time. My intent has been to preserve both their emotional impact and historical meaning, so that readers feel not only informed, but connected to the spirited people of that pioneering era.

'Along the tracks of Cobb and Co.—The Western Run' (Brisbane, Toowoomba, Roma & Charleville) continues the story of this great enterprise as it reached into outback Queensland. This book is dedicated to the memory of Kenneth Victor and Mavis Rosa Johnson. The Johnson brothers (including Ken's father), and their father, Henry John Johnson, were among the early pioneers in the district of Roma—a horse change along the western track. Other change stations along the western run of Cobb and Co., from Brisbane, included Drayton, Toowoomba, Dalby, Condamine, Yuelba, Surat, Roma, and Charleville.

Roma and its surrounding district has a rich history of oil and gas, as told at *The Big Rig*, where the 'Lenroy' Old Slab Hut is located—a reminder that some felt "the times were better, in the days of Cobb and Co. (G. M. Smith), with the dust of bush roads and the sweet odors of ferns and eucalypti, caught on the dewy breath of early morning."

I acknowledge that this book does not explore the deep cultural history of Australia's First Peoples or their interactions with others during this period of colonisation.

Authenticity has been maintained throughout. Spelling, punctuation, and grammar appear as they do in the original sources—features that, in themselves, help tell the story of change over time. The evolution of photography, including the availability and quality of images, is also evident.

Acknowledgement of Country

We acknowledge the Traditional Custodians of the land
on which the Cobb and Co. stage coaches travelled.
We pay our respect to Elders past, present and emerging,
and extend our deep respect to all Aboriginal and Torres Strait Islander Peoples.

TITLES

Book 1
Along the tracks of Cobb and Co. —The Great Northern Road
(Tenterfield to Warwick)

Book 2
Along the tracks of Cobb and Co. —The Western Run
(Brisbane, Toowoomba, Roma & Charleville)

Book 3
Along the tracks of Cobb and Co. —The New South Wales Headquarters
(In & Around Bathurst)

Book 4
Along the tracks of Cobb and Co. —Back to the Beginning
(Victoria & the Goldfields)

Book 5
Along the tracks of Cobb and Co. —Cobb's Coach Drivers

Book 6
Along the tracks of Cobb and Co. —The Roaring Days !
(Amusing Anecdotes & Tales of Grit and Graft)

Book 7
Along the tracks of Cobb and Co. —Queensland
(Brisbane & Beyond) (Release date ... late 2025)

Print | Audiobooks | eBooks
Copyright by Hazel T. Johnson

First Edition May 2022, Reprinted July 2022 & April 2023, Second Edition April 2024, Reprinted July 2025

Content mainly courtesy of Trove (The National Library of Australia) and their many partners including State Library of New South Wales, State Library of Queensland, State Library of Western Australia, and State Library of Victoria. Photographs taken before 1955 and maps created before 1955 are out of copyright (Australian Copyright Council). Thanks to the other contributors of photos and/or information, to assist in the telling of part of the story of Cobb and Co. in Australia. Spelling, punctuation and grammar as per historical sources. Every attempt has been made to ensure the correct use and acknowledgement of all sources. The information in this book is by no means exhaustive. Corrections and/or contributions welcome for the next edition. Book cover image: Cobb & Co. Southport coach, ca. 1900 – Courtesy State Library of Queensland.

Available from www.cobbandcotracks.au or local distributors

Further contact: email dvhtjohnson@gmail.com; Mobile phone +61 417984455

ISBN 978-0-6459759-3-2

This book was printed by: IngramSpark

Typeset in Garamond

Contents

4	Author's Note
8	**Chapter One:**
	Cobb and Co. begins
20	**Chapter Two:**
	Cobb and Co.—a 'loose confederation of proprietors'
26	**Chapter Three:**
	Brisbane—the birth of Queensland and mail conveyance
40	**Chapter Four:**
	Onto Toowoomba and Drayton
54	**Chapter Five:**
	The western mail run
	Mail conveyance to the west
	First Stage—Drayton to Dalby
	Second Stage—Dalby to Condamine
	Third Stage—Condamine to Surat
	The western mail run altered
70	**Chapter Six:**
	Roma—a longer stop
	Early Roma intelligence Roma's oil and gas
	The Big Rig & 'Lenroy Old Slab Hut'
	Resident families 'Lenroy'
	Other Roma landmarks
106	**Chapter Seven:**
	Charleville—a coach building town
116	**Chapter Eight:**
	Beyond Charleville
124	**Chapter Nine:**
	From coaching to motor buggies
133	**The Days of Cobb and Co.**
134	**Appendices**
144	**Reference List**

67

130

Chapter One

Cobb and Co. begins

THE NEAR-SIDE LEADER
By Will. H. Ogilvie

When the gear is on the horses and the knotted trace-chains hooked;
When the last bale's on the waggon and the ropes are twitched and tied;
When the brakes are off the big wheels and the waybills safely booked,
    You can see the old gray leader with his wise head turned aside.
        Does a memory come o'er him
        Of the long, stiff road before him,
With the lead-chains never slackened as he holds his team to work,
        Through the box-flats and the gidyeas,
        Ninety miles of plain and ridges,
To the white-railed Darling bridges and the silver roofs of Bourke?

(The Bulletin, Verse 1, 6 Nov 1897, p.5)

Enduring emblem of Australian life

"The arrival and departure of the coaches from the post office were my excitement of the day ... I envied all dwellers in country places, as the townward-borne vehicles,

with the dust of bush roads and the sweet odors of ferns and eucalypti, caught on the dewy breath of early morning,

still clinging to their wheels and furniture, came dashing round the corner into Bourke-street with a sort of surge or wave of swinging traces, splinter bars and other equine tackle, and with an abundant noise and rattle infinitely inspiriting, pull up at the post-office ... The outgoing mails are a nucleus of delightful bustle and confusion, and among their crowd of eager, anticipative, anxious passengers, are many interesting diversities of character." (A Holiday Ramble on the Yarra Track, 29 Jan 1881, p.1)

By the late 1800s, Cobb and Co. had become an enduring emblem of Australian life. In 'A Holiday Ramble on the Yarra Track', J. W. Curtis continues to paint a vivid picture: "Who among all our friends and readers is not familiar with that most ubiquitous colonial institution, 'Cobb and Co.'s coach,' a mode of travelling whose singularities and excellences of tone, form, and color constitute one of the most vividly impressing pictures of Australia travel? ... The light tenor and alto rattle of chain and harness ... the beat of equine footfalls for a bass ... the swish and sharp crack of whip, all blend to the sympathetic ear into a natural music—an audible exponent of the poetry of motion ... The driver himself appears to have merged his identity in the vehicle he presides over ... He is, on the box, not a man, but part of a mighty system." (A Holiday Ramble on the Yarra Track, 29 Jan 1881, p.1)

Early coaches

Yet decades earlier, long before Cobb and Co.'s golden era, "stage coaches were introduced to New South Wales before the settlement of the Port Phillip district had begun, and in January 1832, there were nine coaches plying from Sydney to various inland towns ... when Melbourne and Geelong were founded, an early attempt was made to connect these two hamlets ... The absence of made roads seems to have defeated the project ... It was not until the opening of the goldfields in 1851 gave rise to a steadily increasing stream of traffic to the interior that coaching days really began in Victoria ... pioneers on the road ... James Watt ... James Elijah Crook ... Ryland John Howard." (Cobb and Co., 20 Jun 1922, p.13)

Imported English coaches proved ill-suited to bush conditions: "British or English style coaches ran in the colonies in Australia with little success, as the coaches were too rigid and heavy for the bush tracks." (An Historical Magazine, 4 Mar 1911, p.19)

Nevertheless, Australia's coaching history stretches further back still. As noted in 1923: "A line was established by Hyland in 1814 ... The first Royal Mail coach ran on March 19th, 1831 ... from the Rose and Crown Inn ... to the Woolpack, at Parramatta." (Old Coaching Days, 15 Jun 1923, p.3) Over time, a network of early coaching proprietors emerged across the colonies: "Charles Henry Jones on the south line, Crane and Roberts, Mylecharane and Elliott ... Nowland Bros. and Gill Bros ... James Bevan and Co. on the Beechworth line; Bill and Deakin, and Howard, with the 'Argus' line ... Samuel Page was the colossus of coaching [in Tasmania] ... Mrs. Cox ... W. Chambers [in South Australia] ... J. Rounsevell ... Hill and Fuller ... Sydney Kidman and James Nicholas [in Western Australia]." (The Contributor, 25 Nov 1908, p.1405)

Goldfields

Victoria was proclaimed a separate province in 1851, as noted in Proeschel's Atlas of Australasia (1863)—a development that aligned with rising transport demands spurred by the gold rush. F. A. Byrne recalled: "To the present generation of Australians the name of Cobb and Co is only a memory ... When gold was discovered in Victoria, in 1851 ... the only means of conveyance ... was by paying a carrier so much per head for the carrying of the passengers' swags and tools, the men walking ... and camping out at night ... The average daily distance was 25 or 30 miles, and for this each man was charged £3 ... The first regular conveyance was inaugurated in 1852 by ... Emanuel King ... a large two-wheeled spring van, drawn by three horses, two leading abreast, and one in the shafts. Light swags only were taken with passengers. There were no changes of horses on the road, and the fare to Forest Creek (Mount Alexander) — a distance of 74 miles — was £5. About the middle of 1853 a change came over this mode of transit." (The Contributor, 25 Nov 1908, p.1405)

Earlier that year, Freeman Cobb arrived in Australia. He was "an American, born near Boston ... being 35 years of age, he arrived in Melbourne ... in order to see what could be done in the coaching line, in the, then, terra incognita of Australia." (Cobb & Co., 5 May 1875, p.4)

Cobb was followed by "James Swanson, John Lamber, and John M. Peck, men who had been in the same employ as himself, and who he had induced to try their fortunes in this new land." (Cobb & Co., 5 May 1875, p.4)

Initially, Cobb worked hauling goods from Liardet's (now Port Melbourne) to the city. However, the route across the swamp between Emerald Hill (modern-day South Melbourne) and the river was such a quagmire that their wagons often sank up to the hubs. The conditions were so discouraging that the effort was eventually abandoned. They advised their principals in the United States [Adams and Co.] against the carrying business, but told them that there was a good opening for a real up-to-date line of coaches to the diggings ... the United States companies turned down the coaching proposition.

Cobb and Co. formed

Following this, George Francis Train, who later recalled: "I told Freeman Cobb, who was then with Adams and Co., that I wanted him to start a line of coaches between Melbourne and the gold-mines, a distance of about sixty miles. I advanced the money for the enterprise, and a line was established, the first in Australia … These were the first coaches seen in that continent." (My Life in Many States and in Foreign Lands, 1902, pp.133–134)

By January 1854, a new firm [Cobb and Co.] entered the coaching scene. "It was not long before American enterprise invaded the field of passenger conveyance. A company of American Californians, says G. F. Train, in a letter dated December 16, 1853, have started a line of passenger waggons (American, of course, made at Concord) to Bendigo; another party have two teams running from Geelong to Ballarat; and some Cape Cod folks are doing a good business with some Yankee coaches between Sandridge and Melbourne." (Cobb and Co., 20 Jun 1922, p.13)

As clarified by Harry H. Peck, "the names of Cobb's three original partners ... were John Lamber, James Swanton, and John Murray Peck (my father) ... they gave up [hauling wagons] ... and began coaching on the Bendigo road on January 30, 1854. Within twelve months Lamber retired, and Arthur Blake came into the partnership." (Old Coaching Days, 10 Jun 1922, p.7)

First advertisement

"Advertisement in The Argus, Melbourne, of January 30, 1854:—AMERICAN TELEGRAPH LINE OF COACHES. Daily communication between Melbourne, Forest Creek and Bendigo. Cobb and Company beg to announce ... The vehicles intended to run are the new American coaches, recently imported, and acknowledged to be the easiest conveyances in the colony." (Cobb and Co., 20 Jun 1922, p.13)

These vehicles were distinctive, though not flawless. As Lovell Smith observed: "The vehicles thus advertised were light Concord coaches, round-bodied, and handsomely upholstered. That they were not suitable for winter traffic ... as the year wore on the service was suspended, and was not resumed until spring ... By the end of 1855 Cobb and Company had two booking offices in Bourke Street ... The heyday of coaching in Victoria was ... near at hand; but Freeman Cobb appears to have been satisfied with the measure of success he had achieved, and was preparing to return to his native land." (Cobb and Co., 20 Jun 1922, p.13)

Indeed, Cobb was soon farewelled with gratitude: "We have much pleasure in learning that a complimentary dinner is to be given to this gentleman on his departure from the colony." (Advertising, 23 May 1856, p.3) Interestingly by 1863, "the city of Melbourne was lighted by gas." (Proeschel's Atlas of Australasia, 1863)

Great pioneer—Hiram Crawford

"Any reference to the early days of coaching in Victoria, or to the history of Cobb and Co. in Australia, would be incomplete unless mention was made of those two great pioneers of the road, Hiram Crawford and James Rutherford… Hiram Crawford ran coaches to Beechworth or on the Sydney road just about the time, or even a little before, Cobb and Co. began to Bendigo Though the big firm, or one of its numerous successors, afterwards took over the main Sydney road line. Mr. Crawford stayed longer in the coaching business in Victoria (fully sixty years altogether), than any of the original Americans, carrying on pretty well right up to his death only a few years ago. Many lines ran out of Albury Wodonga, Wangaratta, and Beechworth, under the titles of Crawford and Co., or Crawford, Connelly, and Co …

Great pioneer—James Rutherford

James Rutherford did more to extend and spread the name and fame of Cobb and Co. throughout Australia than any other man. He joined the firm in 1862 and at once pushed out to the centre of New South Wales, accompanied by three other partners of the firm—Walter Hall … Witney, and Bradley. Mr. Rutherford, who was a fine organiser early established a huge emporium for the firm at Bathurst, where they built their own coaches and made their own harness ... He soon carried the banner of Cobb and Co. right throughout almost the whole of New South Wales and Queensland.

Within a few years the interests of the firm were divided, A. W. Robertson and John Wagner retaining the Victorian lines and the Western portions of New South Wales as far north as Wilcannia, and James Rutherford and his Bathurst confrers taking all the rest of New South Wales and all Queensland." (Old Coaching Days, 10 Jun 1922, p.7)

In Queensland especially, Rutherford's leadership was widely acknowledged. As recorded: "Mr. Rutherford points out the work which Cobb and Co. have done in Queensland for the past forty years, from the time when they came to the rescue of Brisbane by establishing the coach service between this city and Ipswich. Mr. Rutherford was at that time manager, and continued in the position until 1881, when the concern was formed into a company ... He refers to the pioneer work which the company did in opening up communication through all the Downs country, until they were superseded by the railways.

When the Gympie rush broke out in later years, and there was a feeling that the capital might be removed to Maryborough, the Government of the day met Mr. Rutherford, and at their desire he undertook to make a flying survey of the road to Gympie himself, and this was eventually done, and communication opened up.

Again, when Croydon broke out, at the request of the P.M.G. of that day, communication over what was considered to be impossible country was opened up by the company from the field to Normanton; and when trouble in securing coastal communication afterwards followed, the company again acted as pioneers, and opened up a road from Georgetown to Herberton, thus saving people about eight days' time in reaching Brisbane.

A lot of the work, Mr. Rutherford points out, was not done for pay, and throughout he and his fellows were actuated by their interest in the State and their desire to push it forward." (What Cobb and Co. have done for Queensland, 16 May 1902, p.6)

By the 1890s, the scope of Cobb and Co.'s operations was enormous. As reported: "Twenty years ago ... the operations of the firm were nothing short of enormous. As coach and buggy builders they did a business the many ramifications of which extended almost from end to end of the eastern coast. As coaching contractors they harnessed 5000 horses a day alone, employed, directly and indirectly, some thousands of hands, and paid in wages the startling sum of over £200,000 a year, the while their contracts for the mails were of such an extensive character that they ran into £100,000 a year at least.

As squatters, too, the business which they did was on a corresponding scale; the properties worked by them extended over three colonies whilst, as mining men, they enterprised in gold, silver, copper, iron, and coal; and, as one of a syndicate, established the Lithgow iron works, which at one time paid in wages over £3000 a month ... As contractors with the Government, they did a vast amount of railway constructing, and it was they who built that difficult line from Glen Innes to Tenterfield in this colony, the heaviest railway contract that ever was let." (Cobb and Co., 17 Nov 1894, p.1017)

Two years later, it was "estimated that the great firm of Cobb and Co., who own pastoral properties in New South Wales and Queensland, shore this year nearly a million of sheep. Mr. Rutherford, the managing partner, has his head quarters at Bathurst, but he is seldom at home. One week he is in Western Queensland, the next on the Lower Macquarie; a few weeks after at Coombing Park ; and then at Bathurst or Dubbo. Besides being 'shearers of a million fleeces'—to use the words once used by Lord Beaconsfield, when talking of Australian squatters—Cobb and Co. own between 20,000 and 30,000 head of cattle." (Cobb and Co., 20 Oct 1896, p.4)

Meanwhile, the "Victorian assistant Government Statist estimates the population of Victoria on 31st December, 1895, at 1,181751, an increase of 7751 in two years. The excess of births over deaths during that period was 40,000, so that really 32,255 more people must have left the colony than have arrived in it." (Cobb and Co., 20 Oct 1896, p.4)

In 1907, Rutherford's personal story was still being celebrated: "James Rutherford is an American by birth, and an old and energetic colonist. He was born in ... New York State, in August 1827, so that he is now in his 81st year. He came to Victoria in the 'roaring fifties' after a variety of callings, including that of a digger, he joined the firm of Cobb and Co., then active in Victoria and came to New South Wales in 1861 as managing partner. He went to Queensland in connection with the same big business ... For over 40 years Mr Rutherford has resided at Bathurst where he is recognised as a sterling citizen and thorough worker. There is a happy anecdote told of one of Mr Rutherford's trips to his native land.

> Passing through a small town he saw outside a little harness-maker's shop a set of harness which took his fancy. It was just suitable for Cobb and Co. in Australia. Entering, he asked the harness-maker the cost, and being told, fairly astonished the man, who was in a very small way of business by giving him an order for 350 sets.

At one time Cobb and Co. had at any hour of the day 5,000 horses in harness." (James Rutherford, 22 Dec 1907, p.11)

Sadly, in 1911, "News was received (says Friday's Sydney 'Daily Telegraph') of the death of Mr. James Rutherford, at Mackay (Q.) from bronchitis, after a very short illness. Mr. Rutherford had reached the age of 84 years, but preserved to that unusual period of maturity physical and business activities of such a marked character that no fear of his sudden demise was entertained by those with whom he was intimately connected ... the death of a man on his annual health trip to enjoy the milder winter of the tropics who ... controlled immense business affairs ... came as a shock ... to whom James Rutherford represented what, seemed to be a perennial benevolent and business fixture. The deceased gentleman's connection with the famed Australian firm of Cobb and Co. induces many thoughts associated with exploring and pioneering enterprises in Australia, with a name ... held almost more than human ... which carried the light wheel tracks of the mail coach over routes unknown, and unsuspected by even the Myall. It is said of Jim Rutherford that he was faced with the problem of carrying a mail over an inaccessible range ...

> picked out what looked to be the most difficult ... whipped up his horses, and with the remark, 'The road's over there, blazed the track for vehicle and railroad traffic for ever after ...'

With the most indefatigable energy, untiring industry, and extraordinary success, he devoted himself to the organisation of the business of mail carrying in New South Wales and Queensland ... it is said of Cobb and Co., that is, of Mr. Rutherford ... that it opened roads where never else our railways would have penetrated ... He was a devout churchman ... an ardent protectionist ... believed that the future of this country depended upon the development of its industries ... Mr. Rutherford has been one of the most prominent pastoralists in New South Wales and Queensland ... owned Buckinguy Station ... Murrumbidgee Station ... Wyagdon ... his estate at Hereford, near Bathurst ... In Queensland his properties consist of Burrenbella ... Connemarra ... Aubathalla ... Davenport Downs ... and lngledoon ... All those properties have been worked on the most scientific basis ... the C.O.B. wool has more than once topped the London market." (Australian Pioneer, 19 Sep 1911, p.6)

However, by 1922 "the Queensland firm of Cobb and Co. (the really true successors of the original firm of 1857 in Victoria) are advertising the giving up of the business by the selling of their existing lines in piecemeal. Of the original four partners, John Murray Peck was the only one to really adopt Victoria as his home. 'Johnny' Lumber, died in San Francisco some twenty-five years ago. Mr. Swanton in New Zealand, and Mr. Cobb in South Africa." (Old Coaching Days, 10 Jun 1922, p.7)

Railway expansion

During this time, the railway network had been rapidly advancing. As recorded decades earlier: "First Victorian railway opened, 1854 ... First New South Wales railway opened, 1855." (Pugh's Queensland almanac, directory and law calendar, 1864, p.18) By the 1890s, government interest in railway development intensified. In 1895, Judge Casey reported, "It is a function of the rail to develop traffic ...

I travelled over a thousand miles of railway in each of the colonies ... the carriages ... marvellously clean ... admirably constructed ... no jolting ... the lighting by gas is a great boon ... on the narrow gauge lines in Queensland the trains could travel at ... forty miles an hour." (Queensland Railways, 31 Jul 1895, p.6)

During the 1910s, expansion continued. According to a government release: "The Minister for Works (Mr. Cann) has had prepared ... a railway map ... Lines Constructed Since October, 1910: Moree to Mungindi ... Maitland to Taree ... Cooma to Nimmitabel ... Parkes to Peak Hill ... Lines Under Construction: Taree to Grafton ... Dubbo to Werris Creek ... Nimmitabel to Bombala ... Line Authorised: Coonabarabran to Burren Junction." (New Railways, 17 Dec 1915, p.8)

By 1919, railway improvements were still ongoing: "Queensland Railways... On and after Monday, 20th January ... Brisbane and Bundaberg ... Toowoomba and Roma ..." (Queensland Railways, 19 Jan 1919, p.3)

But "the growth of the railway system... meant, of course, the gradual disintegration of the coaching business. Main routes were abandoned, and country lines shrank to the position of short feeders to the railway ... The booking office at coaching glories of Bourke-street was closed in 1890, and eight years later Robertson, Wagner, and Company passed out of existence. To-day the name of Cobb and Company, as far as the directory tells us, survives in but one country township." (Cobb and Co., 20 Jun 1922, p.13)

1881 Outside Cobb's Office,
Bourke-street – The Australasian Sketcher with
Pen and Pencil, 17 Dec 1881, p.401

ca. 1890 Bourke St., Melbourne – Courtesy National Library of Australia

ca. 1880s Hereford, Bathurst – Courtesy Bathurst Historical Society

ca. 1912 Looking west along Malop Street, there is a Cobb & Company coach
in the foreground, Geelong – Courtesy Museums Victoria

ca. 1882 Cobb and Co. coach at W.H. Collis' Royal Hotel at Curraweena, a change station
for Cobb & Co. (Arthur Laycock) – Courtesy National Library of Australia

15 Pre-1915 Graham and Smith 'The Fixit Shop', coach factory, Meredith (L. Haddon) – Courtesy Museums Victoria

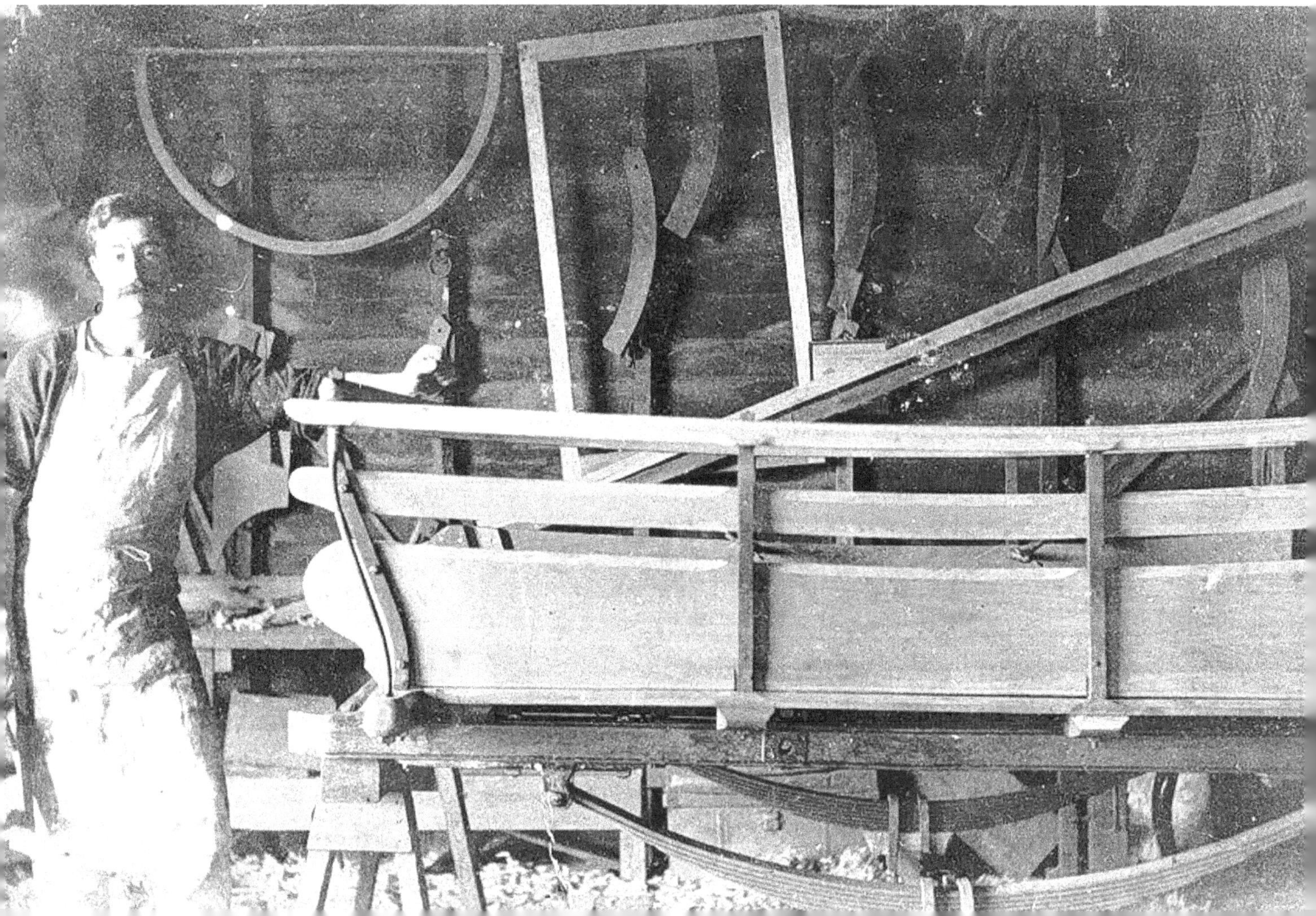

Pre-1910 A man with a carriage which is under construction, Meredith – Courtesy Museums Victoria

ca. 1895 A Cobb and Company stagecoach in a country town, NSW, there is a gas light in the background – Courtesy Museums Victoria

ca. 1900s Horsedrawn Vehicle with Passengers, Lorne (William S. Anderson) – Courtesy Museums Victoria

ca. 1872 Cobb's Camp Hotel, Woombye – Courtesy State Library of Queensland

Cobb & Co. Mail Coaches at a change station in Western Queensland – Courtesy National Archives of Australia

ca. 1866 Holmes railway camp on the Toowoomba Range – Courtesy State Library of Queensland

ca. 1910 Railway tunnel cutting through the hill in the Main Range area – Courtesy State Library of Queensland

1865 Opening of Queensland's first railway, Ipswich to Grandchester – Courtesy State Library of Queensland

ca. 1888 Front entrance of Roma Street Railway Station, Brisbane – Courtesy State Library of Queensland

Chapter Two

Cobb and Co.- a 'loose confederation of proprietors'

THE NEAR-SIDE LEADER.
By Will. H. Ogilvie

Just a whisper from his master and he leans upon the weight,
And the twenty browns behind him touch the collar when he moves,
Then the whip rings out a warning, and the undercarriage grates,
And they bend their backs and lift her from the well-worn loading grooves.
So they open up the tourney, and she starts her long, rough journey
Over ninety miles of noonday and the evenings in between,
And the station gates have freed her,
With the station men to speed her,
And it's 'Buckle down, my leader, on the road you've often been!'

(The Bulletin, Verse 2, 6 Nov 1897, p.5)

Cobb's three original partners

"Mr. Harry H. Peck writing in the Melbourne 'Age.' says... I would like to correct in one or two particulars ... the names of Cobb's three original partners ... were John Lamber, James Swanton, and John Murray Peck (my father). They were with Freeman Cobb ... on the Bendigo road ... Within twelve months Lamber retired, and Arthur Blake came into the partnership." (Old Coaching Days, 10 Jun 1922, p.7)

Cobb and Co. changed hands

Note: For an in-depth analysis, refer to 'Along the tracks of Cobb and Co. - Back to the Beginning'.

THOMAS DAVIES

"The entire plant—coaches, horses, stabling in various parts of the colony—were owned by Thomas Davies, who in 1856, I think, or early in 1857, sold the lot for £60,000... but Mr. Davies... did not succeed in making any adequate returns for himself." (Notes and Queries, 12 Sep 1885, p.19)

ALEXANDER WALKER & WATSON AND HEWITT

"The business of Cobb and Company changed hands twice during the latter part of 1857, Davies selling out to Alexander Walker in September, and Walker parting with it to Watson and Hewitt about a month later ... followed by a division of interests which laid the foundation of that 'loose confederation of proprietors'." (Cobb and Co., 20 Jun 1922, p.13)

SWANTON, BLAKE, AND COMPANY & F. B. CLAPP AND CO.

"Swanton, Blake, and Company had taken over the Bendigo line, and F. B. Clapp and Company, the line to Ballarat; while Watson and Hewitt ... took up the running to Beechworth ... includes 250 horses, and seventeen or eighteen coaches, the price paid being £7,250." (Cobb and Co., 20 Jun 1922, p.13)

"Swanton and Blake are said to have been members of the original 12 partnership of Cobb and Company... F. B. Clapp... founded the Melbourne Omnibus Company ... later established the cable tramway system of the metropolis... his son... now holding office as chairman of the Victorian Railways Commissioners." (Cobb and Co., 20 Jun 1922, p.13)

"The business fell into the hands of Cyrus Hewitt and George Watson ... It was carried on by them until 1860, when it fell into the hands of Robertson and Britton." (The Contributor, 25 Nov 1908, p.1405)

VICTORIAN STAGE COMPANY

"After Mr. Cobb returned to the United States, and the business was sold to Thomas Davies, my father followed him and ... was largely instrumental in forming a new company ... the Victorian Stage Company ... carried on under the old name of Cobb and Co." (Old Coaching Days, 10 Jun 1922, p.7)

"The business fell into the hands of a company, comprised principally of coach agents, drivers, etc., calling themselves the Victorian Stage Company, but their reign was also very short, as disorganisation was quickly caused through there being too many bosses. All this time the name of Cobb and Co. had been retained." (The Contributor, 25 Nov 1908, p.1405)

ROBERTSON, BRITTON AND CO.

"We may note the appearance of the scene of Robertson, Britton, and Company about the middle of 1861... The following year the name of this firm was altered to Robertson, Wagner, and Company ... maintain[ing] the connection of Cobb and Company with the metropolis for more than thirty years." (Cobb and Co., 20 Jun 1922, p.13)

ROBERTSON, WAGNER, AND CO.

"In 1860 Robertson and Britton had it, but Britton soon went out, and Robertson, Wagner, and Co, came upon the scene. (They remained till 1901.)" (Cobb and Co., 18 Jun 1918, p.4)

"Robertson, Wagner and Co ... extended their business in every direction... Crane and Roberts sold their plant... for £16,800... Cobb and Co. extended their operations to the western road... quickly defeated Nowlan Bros... The enormous proportions to which the business had grown may be estimated by the fact that in the year 1867 they were ... in receipt of £95,000 per annum in mail subsidies" (The Contributor, 25 Nov 1908, p.1405)

"Mr John Wagner ... made a start in that direction in 1852, and a few years later had established several lines about Geelong. He went into partnership with Messrs Hewitt and Co ... Later Mr Wagner joined Mr A W Robertson in establishing the firm of Robertson and Wagner, coach proprietors and the new firm bought up several coaching lines ... This was ... before the introduction of railways, and the firm carried the mails for many years, the lines of coaches all being run under the title of Cobb and Co's ... The partnership was dissolved by Mr Robertson's death in 1896." (Death of Mr. John Wagner, 28 Jan 1901, p.7).

"New South Wales was invaded, and the firm of Cobb and Co. consisted of A. W. Robertson, John Wagner, J. Rutherford, Walter Hall, W. Franklin Whitney, W. Bradley and R. Brunig. The firm rapidly acquired coach lines ... there by controlling all the main roads in New South Wales. Shortly afterwards it exploited Queensland." (Cobb and Co., 18 Jun 1918, p.4).

MEIGS AND ANDERSON

"In the middle sixties Meigs and Anderson, and Watson and Hewitt carried the name of Cobb and Company into Gippsland." (Cobb and Co., 20 Jun 1922, p.13)

RUTHERFORD, WHITNEY, AND CO.

"Eventually I formed a company to buy him [Freeman Cobb] out. The partnership was as follows:—James Rutherford, one share; John Wagner, one share; A. W. Robertson, one share; B. and C. Robertson and Pollock, one share; Walter R. Hall and W. F. Whitney, one share.

The purchase money was £23,000—£5000 in cash and the balance in promissory note, and I was appointed manager at £25 a week. Within six months all liabilities were paid off, and we never looked back." (The Founder of Cobb and Co., 5 Dec 1924, p.3)

"Went to Sangate, and was as busy as possible getting our plant started for the Lachlan. It consists of 10 coaches, 103 horses, and two feed waggon, and is in charge of Colin Robinson … Tomorrow I sail for Sydney, but hope to return in three months. Please address, J. Rutherford, Bathurst" (The Founder of Cobb and Co., 5 Dec 1924, p.3)

"In about 1870 the firm split up, and spheres of operation were agreed upon. Robertson and Wagner took Victoria; the Echuca, Deniliquin, Hay, Booligal, and Wilcannia road, and west of it. Rutherford, Whitney, and Co. took North-Western New South Wales, and went into South-West Queensland; while a company was formed to operate in Queensland, with Mr. Grant as managing director." (Cobb and Co., 18 Jun 1918, p.4)

Impact of the railways

"The good old days when 'King Cobb' virtually ruled the roads of New South Wales have gone … To-day one meets covered-in buggies painted red and drawn by two scarecrows … carrying her Majesty's mails at about an eighth of the price once paid to Cobb and Co. for the same service … Cobb and Co. have wisely drawn off the roads, or nearly so … The glory of Cobb and Co. was dimmed by the railway." (Cobb and Co., 18 Dec 1897, p.2)

Consequently, the company began divesting its rural holdings: "Sale of Stations. Cobb and Co.'s Properties… the Yowah station in the Warrego district of Queensland … 153 square miles… for £5,600 … The Miranda Downs station … with 9,000 head of cattle, was passed in at £12,000 … Davenport Downs … with 4,000 head of cattle … These properties … are being sold to close the partnership." (Sale of Stations, 26 May 1899, p.2)

By 1902, internal meetings signalled the firm's ongoing challenges: "Cobb and Co.'s Shareholders… a meeting… called in consequence of the recent trouble with the postal authorities… Certain matters… will be submitted to the whole of the shareholders in the company." (Cobb and Co.'s Shareholders, 29 May 1902, p.4)

"Cobb and Co.'s

glories quickly faded with the rapid extension of the railways to the interior of the States.

The great coaching roads were captured by the locomotive … it was decided to float the business into a limited liability company. That was the beginning of the end, and at present, whilst there are a few coaches running in outback districts under the once great name of Cobb and Co., they are but miserable shadows of the past, and have no tangible right to the name." (The Contributor, 25 Nov 1908, p.1405)

In 1912, another chapter closed with the retirement of "Mr. Thomas Gallagher, the well-known general manager of the coaching firm of Cobb and Co. … He leaves the company after thirty-two years' service … He started with the company as a coach-driver … recognised as one of the most capable drivers in the coaching line … By sheer merit and devotion to the service, he made his career so successful that to-day he leaves it … as the nominal head of the company, to enjoy the evening of his life … Though there is no official foundation for the statement, report has it that the death of Mr. J. Rutherford … is a secondary cause of Mr. Gallagher's retirement … It is believed that a reconstruction of the management of Cobb and Co. will now be made." (Messrs. Cobb and Co., 29 Apr 1912, p.6)

Meanwhile, recollections of the company's complex origins continued were again recorded. Writing in 1918, Alexander Wilson wrote "in 1863… Freeman Cobb, J. M. Peck, James Swanson, and Anthony Blake, all Americans, started in Melbourne as coach proprietors… In 1861 New South Wales was invaded… The firm rapidly acquired coach lines run by Crane and Roberts, Ford and Mylecharane and Nowland Bros., thereby controlling all the main roads in New South Wales… Shortly afterwards it exploited Queensland… About 1870 the firm split up, and spheres of operation were agreed upon… Several gentlemen subsequently well known in politics were drivers on one or other of the company's lines… Mr. Alfred Denkin's father was for many years accountant in the Bourke-street, Melbourne, office of the firm… Most of the men mentioned were Canadians." (Cobb and Co., 18 Jun 1918, p.4)

By 1923, Cobb and Co. Brisbane sought to raise additional funds. "As the directors of this company consider that more capital can be profitably used in business, and will, moreover, enable them to buy better advantage … they have offered for public subscription the balance of 20,000 £1 preference shares." (Money Market Searchlight, 29 Nov 1923, p.9)

Finally in 1929, came the end of an era. A journalist captured the fading echoes of Cobb and Co.'s history: "With a merry rattle, trot, trot, clicketty clack, it made the bend into Queen-street, and passed from sight. Such a scene it was away back in 1865, when the first stage coach of Cobb and Co. opened the mail and passenger line from the tiny capital to Ipswich town… Volumes could be written — tales of adventure, gold rushes, bushrangers, brave pioneers… the hardy men who kept the roads open…

brave men and horses that made the bush ring with the rattle, trot, trot, clicketty clack of iron-shod wheel and hoof…

Mr. G. Studdert, last manager and secretary of the company… is busy sorting… documents, papers, and letters; winding-up the last affairs of Cobb and Co., Ltd., once the greatest firm of coach proprietors this continent has ever known… They confirmed a resolution previously passed: That the company be wound-up voluntarily." (Cobb and Co's Coaching Days: Colourful Page of History Closed, 30 Jun 1929, p.23)

n.d. Factory at Charleville – Coaching in Australia a history of the coaching firm Cobb and Co., W. Lees, p.101

1894 Charleville Post Office, the Cunnamulla and Adavale coaches
– Coaching in Australia a history of the coaching firm Cobb and Co., W. Lees, p.49

1903 Side view of Cobb & Co's factory building at Charleville – Courtesy State Library of Queensland

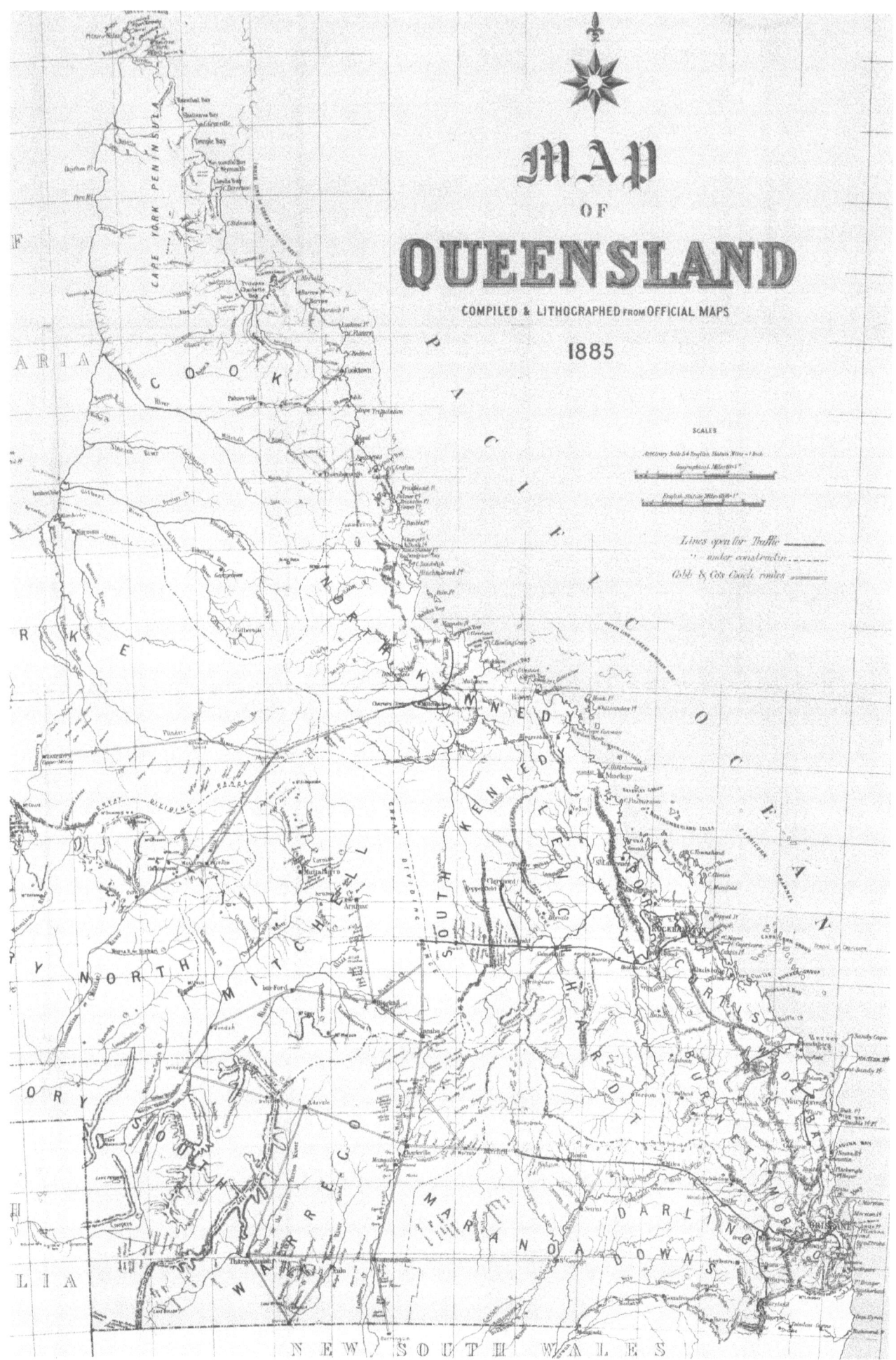
Map of Queensland : compiled and lithographed from official maps, 1885 – Courtesy National Library of Australia

Mr. F. Richards – Coaching in Australia a history of the coaching firm Cobb and Co., W. Lees, p.43

George Francis Train – Geo. Francis Train's Paper, 22 Feb 1884, p.1

Mr. A. W. Robertson – Coaching in Australia a history of the coaching firm Cobb and Co., W. Lees, p.19

Mr. Walter Russell Hall – Coaching in Australia a history of the coaching firm Cobb and Co., W. Lees, p.19

ca. 1920 James Rutherford – Courtesy State Library of Queensland

Cobb & Co., Ltd, Mr. A. Uhl (Chairman) – Coaching in Australia a history of the coaching firm Cobb and Co., W. Lees, 1917, p.31

1872 James Rutherford (T. F. Chuck) – Courtesy State Library of Victoria

Freeman Cobb – The Herald, 2 Jun 1928, p.11

Sir Thomas Brisbane – Picturesque Atlas of Australia, ca. 1886, p.48

Chapter Three

Brisbane-the birth of Queensland & mail conveyance

THE NEAR-SIDE LEADER.
By Will. H. Ogilvie

Now the red dust curls behind her, and the red dust rolls before,
And from shafter up to leader they are sweat from head to hip,
And the good ones take the collar, and the bad ones baulk and bore,
But the grey horse strains the harder every time he bears the whip;
So, by lash and lurid order,
They will swing her through the Border,
With the dust upon her loading making extra weight to pull,
And the drunken township loafer
Staggers blindly from his sofa
Just to see the first team over with the Thurulgoona wool.

(The Bulletin, Verse 3, 6 Nov 1897, p.5)

Major General Sir Thomas Brisbane

In November 1821, Major General Sir Thomas Brisbane arrived in New South Wales with "the annunciation of the arrival from England, on Wednesday last, of the merchant ship Royal George, Captain Powditch, on board of which vessel has arrived, His Excellency Major General Sir Thomas Brisbane, K. C. B. &c. &c. &c. with Lady Brisbane and infant Daughter and Miss McDougall, Sister to Her Ladyship, together with His Excellency's Staff. Upon the vessel coming to an anchor in Sydney Cove, a salute of 19 guns was fired from Dawes' Battery; and immediately afterwards His Honor Lieutenant Governor Erskine proceeded on board, to pay his respects to His Excellencey, and to greet Him on his safe arrival in New South Wales.—His Excellency was pleased to signify his intention of landing on the following morning." (Sydney Gazette, 10 Nov 1821, p.1)

Brisbane's life and legacy were later chronicled in detail by Dr. Cumbrae Stewart. "The Governor ... examination of Moreton Bay ... eventually gave his name to the river discovered there ... Brisbane, from which he took his name, is an estate on the shores of the Firth of Clyde. Through it runs a range of low hills which give the property its name, and if the generally received etymology be correct, the name was originally 'Braes bane,' meaning the fair or the white hills. If this be the true derivation, it presents a peculiar combination of the Lowland Scots word 'braes,' with the Gaelic 'bane.' The people were probably at one time equally at home in both languages ... To the House of Brisbane an heir was born on July 23, 1773. *Every Scotsman*, says Sir Walter Scott, *has a pedigree, and the infant Brisbane was no exception*. His mother was a Bruce of Stenhouse, and Bruce's blood is reckoned the best in Scotland. The child was christened Thomas, and in due course was educated in Edinburgh and London, showing a strong leaning towards mathematics.

At the age of 16 he entered the army ... In 1805 the 69th was ordered to India, and Brisbane's health did not permit him to accompany the regiment. He accordingly went on half pay, and devoted himself to the study of astronomy, building an observatory at Brisbane (Scotland) ... The outbreak of the war with America called him to Canada. He was there when Napoleon escaped from Elba, and did not return until Waterloo had been fought and won. He commanded the second division of the army of occupation, and when it was withdrawn he terminated his military service. Henceforth his interests were mainly scientific. It is said that his desire to examine the southern skies induced him to apply for the Government of New South Wales ...

Brisbane was appointed, and came out in the Royal George, arriving on 7th November, 1821. An interesting light on passage money a hundred years ago is shown by the statement in one of his official letters that his passage alone to this country cost him £1790 more than he was allowed by the Government. This, however, refers to the passage of his household, which included an assistant astronomer ... He did not take over from Governor Macquarie until three weeks later ... One of his first duties was to ... examine the coast of what is now Queensland ... On February 3, 1824, Sir Thomas Brisbane was able to report what had been done. In his own words : It commenced a new era in the History of the Continent of New Holland. He determined to proceed upon the moment the rainy season was over to the establishment of a settlement at Moreton Bay ...

The settlement was formed in August and September 1824. A couple of months later it was visited by the Governor, who was accompanied by Chief Justice Forbes and Mr. John Oxley. They came in the Amity brig, landed at Amity Point and crossed over Stradbroke Island to Point Lookout. Here the Governor made his observations and determined Point Lookout as the most easterly point of Australia. The party ascended the river and stood on the site of the city which was to bear the Governor's name; but not before it had first been called Edinglassie in compliment to the Chief Justice, who was a Forbes of the Edinglassie family." (Founders of Brisbane, 7 Apr 1923, p.11)

In 1825, Brisbane wrote candidly of his experiences and struggles. He said "*The Government of the colony is onerous and peculiar ... I had neither a council to consult, Crown lawyers to advise, nor even a private secretary to assist me ... I do most willingly resign ...* Of high social standing, a victorious general officer, an eminent man of science, he lacked the masterful spirit without which he could not overcome his difficulties. He was too much a gentleman to descend to the level of the warring factions and their coarse and noisy leaders ...

His private life ... was saddened by the death of Lady Brisbane and all their children, and he died on January 27, 1860, in the same room in which he had been born in the old house at Brisbane (Scotland) 87 years before. Before he closed his eyes to earthly things he had learnt that the petty settlement in the South Sea which bore his name had became a Bishop's See, and the capital of the youngest of the Australian colonies." (Founders of Brisbane, 7 Apr 1923, p.11)

Queensland

Development in Queensland accelerated over the next decades. The postal department can be said to have begun in 1842. "White was the first postmaster, the mails being despatched to Sydney by small sailing vessels as opportunity offered." (Coaching in Australia, 1917, p.49) "The post office passed 280,000 letters, 250,365 papers, and 4,456 packets ... Settlement advanced rapidly after 1842." (Geographic History of Queensland, 1895, pp. 12-15) See *Appendix 2.7 1840 Brisbane Town*

In 1849, there was a proposal to increase the price of newspaper transmission. "On the 12th instant the Colonial Secretary, as Chairman of the Committee on the new Postage Bill, brought up the report, and the Bill as amended. Both were ordered, together with the evidence, to be printed. The report recommends an uniform rate of two pence for letters and that, to make up for deficiencies in the Post-office revenue, newspapers shall be charged at the rate of one penny each, instead of at the rate of one halfpenny, as was previously suggested by the great Post-office financier, Mr. Raymond … We have much hope that this boggling 'reform' will be kicked out by the Council." (The News, 24 Sep 1849, p.1)

A decade later, the birth of Queensland occurred in December 1859: "As a result of the agitation for separation, a despatch was received from the Home Government stating that separation had been granted, and that Sir George Ferguson Bowen had been appointed the first Governor. On December 9 Sir George Bowen arrived from England in the warship Cleo, and there was a representative gathering to welcome him when he landed in the Botanic Gardens. A procession was formed, and the Governor was escorted along George-street and Queen-street to Dr. Hobbs' house, which had been taken for three years until Government House could be erected. From one of the verandas the Governor gave a short address to those present and then read the Order in Council granting separation from New South Wales. Judge Lutwyche then swore the new Governor in." (Birth of Queensland, 6 Dec 1925, p.26)

In regard to mail conveyance it was noted, "in case of the separation of the District of Moreton Bay from New South Wales, all Mail Contracts, that include any part of the former District, may cease and determine on one month's previous notice in writing being given to that effect by the Postmaster General." (Conveyance of Mails, 14 Oct 1859, p.2258)

Cobb and Co. establish their presence in Brisbane, Queensland

By 1865 Cobb and Co. had secured a mail contract. "Mr. H. Barnes came to Brisbane to inspect, and shortly afterwards he brought the first turnout, consisting, of 16 coaches in all. The first line was from Brisbane to Ipswich, Cobb and Co securing the mail contract … the firm's coaches were travelling pioneers, opening up routes which afterwards were taken by the railways." (New Books, &c., 1 Sep 1917, p.13)

"Stables were built in Albert-street, on the site now occupied by Fleming and Sons, and on a certain day in the year 1865, the first coach set out on its dash with mails and passengers to Ipswich, with driver Barnes strapped to the box and a team of 12 horses straining at the reins. The opening of the Brisbane-Ipswich line was a great success.

The journey occupied about three hours, there being three changes of horses, and each coach as a rule carried 30 to 35 passengers. The firm received its first setback the following year, when a disastrous fire occurred in the town, and Cobb and Co.'s premises were burnt to the ground. New premises were quickly erected further up Albert-street on the site now occupied by the Queensland Machinery Co. Ltd. Still later the headquarters were built at the junction of Queen-street and Petrie's Bight, near Uhl's saddlery. By this time Cobb and Co.'s lines had been extended far and wide from the capital … Later the Gympie line was added and extended to Maryborough. Then came Brisbane to Sandgate, and one from Beenleigh and Southport, Nerang, Tallebudgera and Murwillumbah, while the Warwick line was extended via Stanthorpe and Maryland to Tenterfield, there joining on with the New South Wales systems, as also at Murwillumbah. Later other lines were extended north and west, and new routes established until Charters Towers, Aramac, Tambo, Emerald, and Roma were all linked up by Cobb and Co's coaches." (Cobb and Co's Coaching Days, 30 Jun 1929, p.23)

Mail conveyance & robbery

1848 – "Jan. 12. — Mail robbery at Bundamba … Feb. 28.— First letter-carrier appointed ; salary £30 … June 2.— First mails despatched to Ipswich by steamer … Nov. 28.— Post office box at South Brisbane established." (Queensland's Half Century 1859 to 1909 Notable Events, 8 Dec 1909, pp.23-37)

1861 – "CONVEYANCE OF MAILS. General Post Office, Brisbane, July 27, 1861. Conveyance being required for the Post Office Mails, from and to the undermentioned places, for one or two years, from the 1st of January, 1862." See *Appendix 3.1 Conveyance of Mails*

MODE OF CONVEYANCE "It will be optional with the parties tendering to propose the mode of conveyance, but on all mails where wheeled vehicles can travel, a preference will be given to carriages licensed for a limited number of passengers. Mails Guards and Postal Inspectors must be conveyed free … no contractor will be bound to travel at a quicker rate than seven miles an hour … a fine of five shillings for every five minutes delay after the specified time of starting … Intending contractors must understand that no excuse for delay will be entertained unless supported by certificates from persons of known respectability." (Conveyance of Mails, 16 Sep 1861, p.6)

1864 – POSTAGE "All letters posted in Queensland must be pre-paid by affixing thereon postage stamps of sufficient value … Iron letter receivers, intended for the receipt of letters only, are fixed at South Brisbane, Fortitude Valley, Kangaroo Point, and Spring Hill … should a packet be posted unpaid … such packet will be sent to the Dead Letter Office, and returned to the writer." (Pugh's Queensland almanac, 1864, pp.120-127)

1866 – "INLAND MAIL SERVICE.—During the year 1866, and part of 1867, some of the mail contracts were not carried out in so satisfactory a manner as heretofore. This was caused, in a great measure, by the depression in the affairs of the colony, which, among others, seriously affected mail contractors; and also to severe drought, especially felt in the westward portion of the colony.

At the commencement of the present year (1869) the contracts mostly terminated, and fresh ones have been entered into ... The contracts of the firm of Cobb and Co. by coach, which now include from Dalby and Condamine to Roma, Toowoomba and Warwick, have been carried out with the greatest regularity ...

The gross number of miles travelled ... for the year 1868 ... will be 950,488 ... The Inland Mail Service now extends from Brisbane, southerly to Nerang Creek; due west to Bulloo Creek beyond the Paroo River, a distance, in a direct line, of 600 miles from Cameron's, on the Warrego. Northward from Cameron's to Charleville, Carrangarra, Alice Downs (on the Barcoo), and Bowen Downs on the Thompson River, and thence to Bowen. From Townsville via Dalrymple, on the Burdekin, to the Flinders River, and thence to Burketown, near the shores of Carpentaria, a distance, by the mail lines, of 1,615 miles. Between these lines and the eastern coast, a network of mail lines intersect one another— in all, a distance of 8,552 miles. Considering the great extent of territory which has to be supplied with postal communication, the many difficulties which have to be contended with ... it is surprising that the mail service is so regularly carried out ... Being fully alive to the anxiety with which persons who are living far from the centres of civilization look forward to the arrival of the mailmen, it has been my endeavour to push out the inland mail service as much as a due regard to expenditure would warrant." (The Queensland Post-office, 26 Jan 1869, p.3)

1869 – "THE QUEENSLAND POST-OFFICE. We make the following extracts from the last report furnished by the Postmaster-General: General Post-office.— The staff of the General Post-office at Brisbane consists of thirty-three persons, including clerks, sorters, and letter carriers; and seventeen at country post-offices, the post-masters of which are attached to the Civil Service; and eighty four other country postmasters. The total number of persons attached to the General Post-office department throughout the colony is one hundred and thirty-six." (The Queensland Post-office, 26 Jan 1869, p.3)

1902 – EFFECTS OF DROUGHT "Cobb and Company Queensland Operations Suspended ... Brisbane, May 12. From Saturday last Cobb and Co.'s coaches throughout the whole of Queensland ceased running. The firm spent £20,000 a year in wages and £22,000 a year on horse feed, and its coaches covered 4,000 miles of road. For a considerable time the Company has been working at a big loss, owing to the drought and the famine prices of feed. The Queensland National Bank now refuses to finance the firm any further ... The Company's office has been deluged with telegrams from commercial travellers who are stranded in the far-off towns. It is feared that many places will not even get necessary food supplies, owing to the stoppage of the coaches. Cobb and Co.'s action in stopping their coaches is creating consternation all over Queensland." (Cobb and Company, Western Mail, 17 May 1902, p.23) Meanwhile "The mails by the services affected by the stoppage of Cobb and Co. are all to hand in the district." (Cobb and Co.'s Coaches., 16 May 1902, p.6) "The Postmaster-General received the following telegram, Cobb writes ... *One of our fellow bondsman is now in Brisbane ... made necessary financial arrangements with our banker ... we are in a position to take the delivery of mails on all routes to-morrow.*" (Queensland Mail Service, 24 May 1902, p.12)

Along the tracks—Brisbane

1884 saw R. E. Jarman & Co. v. Cobb & Co., at the Brisbane House Club Association. "A match took place last Saturday, in Stephens' paddock, South Brisbane. Cobb and Co. gave the boys of the leather a fearful thrashing. 1 innings and 9 runs to spare, think of that. Though good enough to beat Berkley and Taylor one week before, when they face Cobb's eleven, they are not equal to the occasion. How comes this? We will see. Jarman's men went in first, and were all out for the small total of 21—12 of that being made by Stokes and Krist. Cobb and Co. to the wickets then proceeded, and 49 was put up before the last wicket fell. Barnard made 16, not out, and T. E. Shaw 8. Nothing daunted, the leather brethren went in again, but, doleful to relate, they made only 19, and thus the game was at an end. The best bowling was done by Kruck and Uhlman for Cobb's, and Nelson and Armstrong for Jarman." (Brisbane House Club Association, 12 Apr 1884, p.18)

By 1890 Brisbane was "an Episcopal city, and the capital of Queensland, is situated 58 feet above sea-level. On the river Brisbane, which surrounds it on two sides, about 25 miles by water ... from its debouchement into Moreton Bay, one of the largest bays on the coast of Australia ... Brisbane was originally settled in 1825, having been made a penal station by Sir Thomas Brisbane, the Governor at that time of Australia, from whom its name is derived ... In 1842 the colony was opened to free settlers, and from that period the city has made steady progress ... four portions: North Brisbane, South Brisbane, Kangaroo Point, and Fortitude Valley ... Queen Street being the leading thoroughfare ... in George Street ... the post and telegraph office ...

A magnificent iron bridge, called the Victoria, on the lattice-girder principle, with swing openings to allow of the passage of ships, connects North and South Brisbane.

The swing was rarely used, and is now permanently closed ... There is frequent communication with Sydney ... the railway journey occupying about 35 hours ... a regular line carrying mails plies bi-weekly between Brisbane and the northern ports ... There is also regular communication with London by the vessels of the Queensland Royal Mail line ... The shallowness of the river itself, vessels of large tonnage could not come up to the city ... A complete channel of 300 feet wide to upwards of 15 feet at low water, is now available between Brisbane and the Bay. The mail vessels of the Queensland Royal Mail line now regularly come up the river and berth at the wharves ... Brisbane is the terminus of the Southern and Western railway ...

At One Tree Hill, now called Mount Cootha, a large area has been reserved as a public park, a magnificent view is to be had ...

The extension of the city has been much hindered by the hilly nature of the ground ; and the formation of the roads has been attended with a large expenditure of money and labour … Population … census district 51,689." (The Australian Handbook, 1890)

While "the Royal Hotel, in Queen street, dates from the early 60's., and in 1890 it came into note as the starting point, of Cobb and Co.'s coach. The line of coaches to Ipswich had formerly started from Nowlan's Hotel, South Brisbane, but Cobb and Co., whose headquarters were in Albert street, near where Peter Fleming and Co. now have their ware-house, ran the line from the Royal Hotel, across the Custom House ferry to Kangaroo Point." (Old Brisbane Inns, 13 Jun 1922, p.3)

During that same time, the following 'Funny Thoughts' appeared in the Telegraph: "The Brisbane River alligator, which has been playing some queer pranks lately, appears to be an acknowledged fact. The fisherman's yarn of the attack made upon him must, without doubt, be accepted as a true bill—for it is a funny little way those amphibious reptiles have.

The writer once saw a terrible encounter in the north between a snake and an alligator. The latter was lying on the bank of a river with its jaws open when an enormous snake came cruising along, and quick as thought, the alligator swallowed that snake. But his snakely passenger made such a commotion in the internals of the alligator that the scaly saurian was glad to disgorge its prey.

No sooner said than done. The snake returned the compliment and swallowed the alligator, but was just as eager to get rid of the monster in the same way. They kept swallowing and ejecting each other till they got so mixed up they didn't know which was snake and which was alligator.

The end of it was the snake concluded he had changed places and took a header into the river, while the alligator climbed the nearest tree and fancied he was the snake. Some unbelieving folks might doubt this story, but it is quite as true as most snake yarns." Following this was: "*Why Women Dress Well Father: If you paid more attention to cooking and less to dress, my dear, you would make a much better wife.* Daughter: *Yes, Father. But who would marry me!* …

And B. Mountcastle & Sons, of Albert Street, have recently introduced a lightweight white unshrinkable flannel for tennis and cricket shirts, under vests, drawers, &c., which has given the greatest satisfaction." (Funny Thoughts, 10 Mar 1892, p.5)

In May 1897, an incident of considerable public interest was reported in The Telegraph, detailing a dramatic and tragic accident involving a horse in central Brisbane. "About 9 o'clock on Thursday morning (says The Telegraph), an accident happened in Adelaide Street, resulting in the death of a horse, the property of Mr Thomas Bruce. In accordance with his usual custom, Mr Bruce had driven into town to his work at Messrs Stewart and Hemmant's, where he is a manager of a department, and after setting down three other occupants of the trap at the corner of Albert and Adelaide Streets, he was driving along Adelaide Street to the livery stables when he noticed the horse begin to shiver and throw its head back as if to avoid a blow. It seemed as though the animal would reel and fall, and to save possible damage to the shafts, Mr Bruce stopped and took it out. After a few starts and plunges, the horse fell, but again got on its feet, still shivering and apparently in a highly excited condition. Directly afterwards it broke away and dashed along Adelaide Street from opposite the Globe Hotel. First, it collided with the fence of the saleyards and then careered on till it reached the Deposit Bank buildings, where it dashed through the large plateglass window of the shop occupied by Mr Ridge, working jewellery, &c. The window smashed with a great crash, and the horse, rearing, fell backwards into the watertable with a terrible gash in the throat and chest. Death resulted almost immediately. The occupants of Mr Ridge's workshop, along with a young girl who was passing and fled into the shop for safety, had a great fright. Fortunately, no one was hurt either in the shop or in the street." (Strange Horse Accident in Brisbane, 22 May 1897, p.2)

Railway expansion

Back to June 1866, when the expansion of Queensland's railways prompted a reorganisation of Cobb and Co.'s coach schedules to coordinate with the newly opened line to Gatton: "The new railway time-table which is to be in force to-morrow when the line is to be opened for regular traffic to Gatton, will make considerable difference in the coaching arrangements, and it is desirable that travellers should be clearly informed of them. The coach from Brisbane will leave daily at half-past 6 in the morning, and at half an hour after noon. The arrival at Ipswich will be 10 and a quarter to 4. At half-past 10 and at 4 the trains will leave for Gatton, where they will arrive at 1 o'clock and at half-past 6 in the evening. The Toowoomba coaches, which will meet these trains at Gatton, will arrive at Toowoomba at half-past 5 in the evening, and half an hour before midnight." (Cobb and Co's Coaches, 2 Jun 1866, p.4)

Fast-forward to 1921, the question was asked, "Where now are Cobb and Co.'s coaches ? We have still a link with that famous line of coaches in Brisbane. (writes 'Red Gum') I refer to Mr. Hyram Barnes, the venerable and esteemed father of the Hon. W. H. Barnes, the member for Bulimba, and Mr. G. P. Barnes, the member for Warwick. Mr. H. Barnes is now in his 79th year … I had a few words with the veteran 'knight of the whip' … reference was made to the demise of Mr. James Rutherford, with whom Mr. H. Barnes was associated for many years … The days of the bushrangers have happily passed away, but Mr. Hyram Barnes is one of the very few surviving men who, while in charge of coaches, had personal encounters with the rangers …

Mr. H. Barnes introduced Cobb and Co.'s coaches to Ipswich in the year 1865, having bought out Mr. J. Nolan, who, for some years previous, ran the mail coach between Ipswich and Brisbane. Further, Mr. Barnes purchased … the mail coach between Toowoomba and Ipswich … likewise between Toowoomba and Dalby, and subsequently ran Cobb and Co.'s coaches from Dalby and Roma … but since the railways have stretched out into the far country there is very little work for coaches." (A link with Cobb and Co.'s coaches, 28 Sep 1911, p.4)

Exit Cobb and Co.

1920 "Exit Cobb and Co. Brisbane. Sunday. It is reported that Cobb and Co's. large factory will not carry on any more coaching after present contracts have been completed." (Exit Cobb and Co., 20 Dec 1920, p.2)

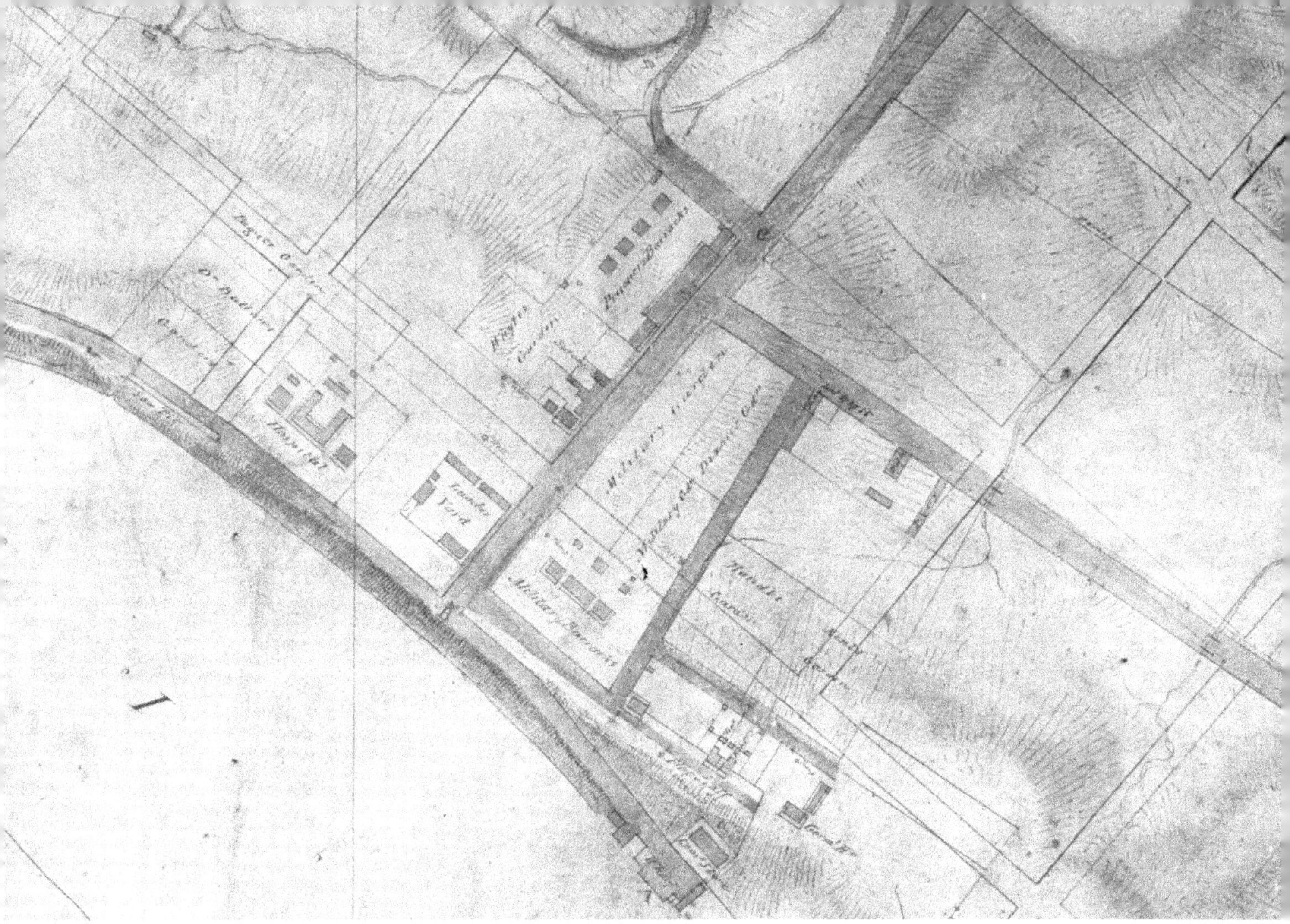

1840 Photograph of map of Brisbane Town – Courtesy The University of Queensland

Watts Family photographs (John Watts Jnr) – Courtesy State Library of Queensland

1850s View of Milton towards Hale Street Cemetery, Brisbane – Courtesy Brisbane City Council Libraries

1859 Showing E. B. Southerden Drapery Stores, Queen Street, Brisbane (Hume Family Collection) – Courtesy The University of Queensland

1893 Panorama of the Brisbane River during the floods – Courtesy State Library of Queensland

1864 Charlotte Street, Brisbane, during the flood – Courtesy State Library of Queensland

ca. 1855 Post Office and Savings Bank, Brisbane – Courtesy Digital Collections, QUT Alumni Collections

ca. 1879 Victoria Bridge from Queen Street, Brisbane – Courtesy State Library of Queensland

1929 Brisbane from Mount Cootha, Brisbane (Herbert H. Fishwick) – Courtesy State Library of Queensland

1868 Cobb and Co coach leaving The Australian Hotel Queen Street Brisbane for Gympie (Geo Thorne on Bot in white, Fred Shaw driver, Inspector Lewis in white, John Hayes boy) – Courtesy Queensland University of Technology

1926 Lovelock family with friends at the waterfall, Mt. Cootha area, Brisbane – Courtesy State Library of Queensland

1862 Observatory Brisbane before Queensland's first railway (John Watson) – Courtesy State Library of Queensland

1860s Daniel O'Brien's Blacksmith shop at Amberley, Ipswich (Brown & Bailey) – Courtesy Ipswich Libraries

ca. 1880s-1900s Rowing race on the Hamilton Reach section of the Brisbane River – Courtesy State Library of Queensland

1899 Gatton College – Courtesy State Library of Queensland

First hotel at Gatton – Courtesy State Library of Queensland

1907 Farmer and his two children in the fields in the Lockyer – Courtesy State Library of Queensland

ca. 1907 Driving along a bush track in the Gatton district – Courtesy State Library of Queensland

Chapter Four

Onto Toowoomba and Drayton

THE NEAR-SIDE LEADER.
By Will. H. Ogilvie

Oh ! the camping by the river when the sun is riding low ;
Oh ! the shifting of the collars and the dropping of the chains ;
And the music of the big bells, as they let the horses go
To their drinking in the river and their feeding on the plains !
So, from camp to camp-fire, daily,
They will battle through Belalie,
Till they leave the plains behind them and the river at their back,
Where the stony hills are showing
There is panting now, and blowing,
But the grey horse keeps them going with the chains that never slack.

(The Bulletin, Verse 4, 6 Nov 1897, p.5)

Train collides with sulky

"When the construction of the Drayton deviation was first proposed, and then during its subsequent building, there was a good deal of foreboding on the part of pessimists regarding the probability of serious consequences arising from the collision of vehicular and train traffic on the level crossings in the city area ... Although information on the subject is very vague and conflicting, the 'Chronicle' has every reason to believe that there was a collision between a sulky and an incoming train at the Russell-street crossing one day this week ... A well-known citizen was driving into town down Russell-street in a four-wheeled sulky drawn by a lively stepping horse. As he approached the crossing, it is alleged that he did not observe the approaching train until he had almost reached the crossing. As his horse was travelling at a fast rate, he saw that if he attempted to pull it up there was the undoubted result that he would collide with the train. Knowing what probable serious results might occur, he decided to take the risk of attempting to cross the line before the train. The horse and part of the sulky got safely across the line, but the engine of the oncoming train crashed into the rear wheels of the sulky, smashing them completely, the occupant being thrown out onto the roadway. So far as can be ascertained, however, he sustained no serious injuries." (Drayton Deviation Accident, 25 May 1918, p.6)

Along the tracks—Drayton (The Springs)

In 1827, after crossing the Main Range, the future Darling Downs was described as "a beautiful and well watered valley, affording abundance of the richest pasturage, and bounded on each side by a bold and elevated range." (Queensland Railway & Tourists' Guide, 1891, p.37) While recorded in 1840 were the "first drays brought over Cunningham's Gap." (Pugh's Queensland almanac, 1864, p.20)

Later that decade, a postal route was established to the settlements on the Downs. "A post office was established at Drayton, one at Limestone (now Ipswich) and a mail service established between, Ipswich, and the Darling Downs." (Coaching in Australia, W. Lees, 1917, p.49) However, at that time "there is no lawyer, doctor, or clergyman." (Queensland Railway & Tourists' Guide, 1890)

By 1847, however, Drayton began to emerge as a focal point for settlement and inland business, although "it is a matter of considerable surprise that the Government have as yet taken no steps to lay out any of the land on the Darling Downs, as village reserves. I was much struck on visting the Downs recently to observe the large amount of business now done at Drayton, a situation well chosen, being the first stage after crossing the main range from the Moreton Bay district. Mr. Stephen Mehan has lately finished a very commodious inn at that locality, and which from experience I can vouch contains every requisite for the creature comforts. The Postmaster, Mr. T. Alford, has also a well built store and dwelling-house ; there is also a blacksmith, wheelwright, and shoemakers' shop, and a couple of medical gentlemen have also recently established themselves in the neighbourhood ; the inhabitants sadly want a tailor to set up amongst them, who would be insured of plenty of work ; in fact, from the increasing traffic on the Downs, from the gradually opening out of the northern country, Drayton, must command a large amount of the inland business." (Moreton Bay, 5 Mar 1847, p.3)

One of the young men working in Mehan's store was William Henry Groom, who would go on to become one of Queensland's most respected public figures. "Few people know that he started to discuss public affairs when a young man as a clerk in Mehan's Store in Drayton ... in 1860 he became Mayor of Toowoomba." (The Gensis of Toowoomba, 7 May 1920, p.6)

Drayton, originally known as 'the Springs,' was formally laid out in 1849 by surveyor J. C. Burnett. "On April 7th, 1848, there was a public meeting at the Downs Hotel, at Drayton, to raise money to sink a town well ... Originally it was known as the 'Springs,' and at one time became an important town ... The native name of Drayton is 'Moyumneura,' literally, 'many tomahawks,' originating in the manufacture of a lot of iron tomahawks by the first Drayton blacksmith, to be given to the [First Nations Peoples] for services rendered or presentation purposes." (Queensland railway & tourists' Guide, A. Meston, 1890, pp.38-39)

It was not until February 2, 1848, that James Powers made history as the first official mailman from the Downs, beginning formal postal deliveries to Brisbane. "It seems remarkable that Drayton continued for practically six years before the first mail man, James Powers, started the first official mail bags to Brisbane on the 2nd of February, 1848. He was the first mailman from the Downs." (The Gensis of Toowoomba, 7 May 1920, p.6)

By the early 1850s, Drayton was establishing the institutions and amenities of a settled community. In 1852, licensing records show: "certificates were issued by the Drayton Bench to the undermentioned persons, viz - Mr. W. Horton, 'Bull's Head' and Mr. David Mehan, 'Downs Inn', Drayton." (Domestic Intelligence, 1 May 1852, p.3) See *Appendix 2.3 1852 Classified Advertising*

Travellers of the era, such as Nehemiah Bartley, captured vivid impressions of the journey into the region. He recalled his approach to Drayton in 1854: "I passed some pretty creeks, with splendid cedar trees, at a camping place; passed a conical hill, with the top cut off flat, on my left ; rode past a hill foot, strewn with boughs of trees, which had been used as drags by descending drays; rode up a sideling cutting, chipped out of the very wall of the Main Range ... Topping this, I came to the green and oozy 'Drayton Swamp' (now Toowoomba), past a tiny cemetery, and got to old Drayton, and put up at the hotel of William Horton ... the 'Royal Bull's Head,' with a parlour, and a style much above those of the wayside inns from Ipswich ...

Opposite was Wm. Handcock's store ... and there was a curious little church, where Canon Glennie preached ; he was not a 'Canon,' then, you know ... on to Warwick ... Such a clean, gravelly, level town, after that broken gully of a Drayton" (Opals and Agates, 1892, p.114).

While Dr. Lang also travelled over the Downs when Drayton was the township, and "he says it was selected because it was the only spot at the time, when trading people and mechanics first desired to settle in the district, that could be had on any terms from their high mightinesses the squatters!

He says it was a most unsuitable site for a town, but this led to the formation of another and rival town called Toowoomba, in the same central part of the country, about 4 miles from Drayton. Governor Sir George Bowen wanted to combine both towns … the suggestion was not adopted … Toowoomba had to rest contented with the more modest position of chief town of the Darling Downs." (Queensland railway & tourists' Guide, A. Meston, 1891, pp.38-39)

Bull's Head Inn

1858 – PUBLIC HOUSE "We had not a drop of rain on the Downs for some months … except of two showers that latterly fell in the vicinity of Drayton … it was confined to the little township … We have at present but one public house between Drayton and Toowoomba, viz., the Bull's Head Inn. I do assure you it is a great acquisition to the place." (Moreton Bay, 5 Apr 1858, p.6)

1857 – "AN OLD-TIME INN. The illustration in your issue of last Monday of the Bull's Head Inn at Drayton, writes Mr. T. Mathewson, awoke in my mind memories of days long past. I remember the building very well in 1857, when Captain Witham was the lessee. The property was owned by Mr. Wm. Horton (who formerly conducted it), but at that time was living privately at the swamp … In the early sixties the Hortons were again occupying the hotel. The Bull's Head was largely patronised by the squatters, but it also had a very money making connection with the rougher sort. For this trade a large bar room was situated at the western end, perhaps 30 by 18 feet in size. At one end were the usual shelves containing the liquors. A counter stretched right across the room and on top of this were hinged shutters, so that the whole could be safely enclosed from the largest part of the room. I learn that during the earlier fifties and forties many a bushman had knocked down a fair sized cheque amid drunken revelry. In '57 I witnessed an entertainment in this bar room, given by a Professor Parker (who was a powerful swordsman) and another, the latter with his banjo and song.

I saw Parker cut the carcase of a sheep in two with one stroke.

Nearly opposite the Bull's Head, but on lower ground, was a hotel, owned by Mr. Stephen Meehan (storekeeper) … After this, the hotel remained unoccupied for a few months, and one dark night about March '58, the alarm of fire was sounded, and I witnessed the whole structure reduced to ashes within half an hour." (An Old-time Inn, 30 Jun 1924, p.10)

1856 – HORSE KNOCKED UP "I feel sorry in having to mention a most flagrant and glaring case … respecting the transit and delivery of the overland mail, via Maitland and New England. The mailman, on arriving at the post office, Drayton … reported to me and other persons that he was compelled to leave three bags, containing letters and papers, behind in the bush ; that he had tied the horse up to a tree on whose back the same were secured, the poor animal being knocked up. I am aware that this has been a severe winter, and forage scarce, yet at the same time a person that undertakes from the government a contract for the transit of mails, ought to furnish, and in fact is bound to provide good cattle to convey the mails safely to their destination. Present contractors are well paid, there being very few in many parts of the colony to oppose them. From what I learn, no blame is to be attached to the mailman ; he does all he can to urge his horses on, in order that he may deliver his mail in due time." (Drayton, 12 Aug 1856, p.3) Mr. William Horton was also proprietor of 'Red Cow' Ipswich. See *Appendix 2.3 Classified Advertising*

1858 – SEPARATION OF MORETON BAY [Brisbane] "On the 23rd November, 1857, the Executive Council … adopted the following Electoral District Scheme for the Colony of Moreton Bay … 5. Town of Drayton (including Toowoomba). Population 528. Members 1." (Separation of Moreton Bay, 28 Apr 1858, p.3)

1859 – ROYAL BULL'S HEAD INN "The application of Mr. William Horton for a license for the Royal Bull's Head Inn, Drayton, was granted." (Adjourned Licenses Meeting, 5 May 1859, p.3)

Along the tracks—Toowoomba

By the early 1860s, Toowoomba was already drawing the attention of travelers making their way across the Range. B. A. Haywood recounted his arrival in 1861. *"At the end of our horse journey in November, 1861, on reaching the top of the Range the scenery was extensive and magnificent, and after descending some-what we came to Toowoomba, where we stayed at Witham's Hotel, and had bronze-winged pigeons for tea. Toowoomba will be a great town. It has a School and Literacy Institute, and lectures are given in the library."* (The Gensis of Toowoomba, 7 May 1920, p.6)

By 1891, the town was widely recognised as an important inland centre. A. Meston described it as "a large and important town, in the centre of one of the best and healthiest agricultural districts in the Colony. It is also one of the oldest towns in Queensland. In the early days it was known as the 'Swamp,' from the wet marsh in the bottom of the valley in which the town is now partly situated. The word 'Toowoomba' is the native name of a small indigenous melon, which grew there in abundance in the days of early settlement … [The First Nations Peoples] belonged to the Gooneeburra or Fire Blacks of the Darling Downs." (Queensland railway & tourists' Guide, A. Meston, 1891, pp.38-39)

When naming the town, Toowoomba avoided suggestions such as Queensborough and Bowenvale. Likewise, Warwick escaped being called Canningtown (The Gensis of Toowoomba, 7 May 1920, p.6)

The local press was established early. "The press was early represented, the Darling Downs Gazette being started by Lyons, at Drayton, on June 11th, 1858.

This paper is now in Toowoomba, its younger rival being the Toowoomba Chronicle, started in July 6th, 1861, by D. Hunt." (Queensland railway & tourists' Guide, A. Meston, 1891, p.398)

In December 1872, the town celebrated Christmas with enthusiasm. Reports from the day tell of busy streets and a lively crowd but the holiday period was also marked by mischief and tragedy. "The town yesterday was all dressed from top to bottom in holiday garments … crowd of pedestrians which thronged our principal street from morning until midnight …

We have reason to believe that our local tradesmen will have cause to designate the Christmas of 1862 as the most profitable they have ever experienced in Toowoomba …

Garden robberies are again coming into fashion … We understand from a gentleman who is one of the first victims that two palings at the lower part of his garden were taken down and an apricot tree, the fruit of which was not ripe, but in fine condition for pies, was completely stripped. Footsteps were seen on the grass, so that the robbing must have been effected early on Monday morning … It is our melancholy duty … to record the sudden death last night of Mrs. Eliza Towell, wife of Mr Thomas Towell, telegraph station-master …" she "had exposed herself freely to the sun … taken suddenly ill …

the cause of death is stated to have been solar paralysis of the brain,

brought on by excessive heat." (Toowoomba Christmas Races, 25 Dec 1872, p.3)

In June 1873, the town experienced its heaviest recorded rainfall. It caused widespread flooding and significant damage "The heaviest rainfall ever recorded in this district occurred on Wednesday morning last … the rain descended literally in torrents, flooding the streets in a manner that was never before witnessed by the oldest inhabitants. The rain was accompanied by a heavy gale of wind, and grave fears were entertained as to the fate of many of the frail wooden buildings erected on the banks of the creeks and water courses at the lower part of the town … Ruthven street, from the corner of Margaret-street to the Post office, was covered with water, while Russell street presented the appearance of a large swift running river … the hurrying waters running over the middle rail of the bridge and flooding Mr Stirling's smithy and the butcher's shop (Mr Hickson's) adjoining. On the west side, the railway grounds were partially flooded. A strong current appeared to be running through the Chinaman's store on the south side of the street … he found himself up to about the waist in water … At Stein's Bridge, James street, a boy who had imprudently attempted to pass from one side to the other was swept through the railing, and with some difficulty was saved from drowning. The dams at the new flour mill (Messrs Neden's) and at Mr Stott's fellmongery establishment were swept away, and several valuable improvements in the Drayton municipality were destroyed … Considerable damage has been done to the growing crops in the neighborhood of the town, the soil having in many instances been completely washed from the roots of the plant … Communication with the outlying districts has in a great measure been suspended, but we fear that grave accounts will arrive by the next mail … The country in the vicinity of Glengallen presented the appearance of a large sea, and the Condamine River was higher by four feet on Wednesday morning than during the great flood of 1864. On the Dalby line, the bridge near the Jondaryan Scrub was rendered unsafe for ordinary purposes, the whole of the foundation having been laid bare … From Cambooya a correspondent writes : We have suffered greatly from the flood. The dam which the Government took over the other day from the proprietors of Eton Vale, and which was constructed at the head of Emu Creek at a cost of about £300, is completely washed away. It was the intention of the Government to form the dam and a portion of the surrounding land into a water reserve, and many homestead selections have recently been made in consequence thereof … I have not seen the Cambooya Creek so high for the last sixteen years. Tyson's washpool, yards, tanks, &c, have all been washed away. Through the courtesy of Mr. Hanna, telegraph station master, we are enabled to give the following measurements of the rainfall in town during the past eight days :- On the 13th, 1.00 inch ; 14th, 0.41 inch ; 15th, 0.22 inch ; 16th, 0.12 inch, 17th, 2.05 inches, 18th, 5.80 inches ; 19th, 0.07 inch, 20th, 0.43 inch, making a total of 10.10 inches - D. D. Gazette" (The Floods in the Toowoomba District, 24 Jun 1873, p.4)

By 1890, Toowoomba had developed further. The town had become a hub of education, health services, and wine production, being "the principal town of the rich district called the Darling Downs. It is situated upon the summit of the Great Dividing Range, 1,921 feet above sea-level, at the head of the Gowrie Creek, a tributary of the Condamine, in the county of Aubigny, electorate of Drayton and Toowoomba … the hotels are numerous … 7 State schools … Roman Catholic school … a grammar school for boys, on a commanding and healthy site overlooking the town, erected at a cost of £10,000, and three seminaries for young ladies … a good hospital—a new building of brick … The streets, public buildings, and many private residences are lit with gas. The town is rapidly extending … There are about 1,000 Germans in the suburbs of Toowoomba, who have vine-yards of more or less extent, and many thousand gallons of wine are annually made … The population of the district … was 9,428." (The Australian Handbook, 1890)

By 1924, changes in transportation were beginning to shape daily life: Writing at the time, 'Kobbi' observed— 'The motor buses' which in the larger cities have come to stay, are already pushing their way well into the suburbs and over the dotted line into the next parish. Distance seems no obstacle, nor for that matter do roads … comercial travellers and pig-buyers now make the regularly journey per petrol bus from Toowoomba to Warwick … It is not difficult to forecast that these city 'coaches' will in due course link up all the scattered towns and hamlets of the closer-settled parts, like the Downs at any rate … in the meantime until the Main Roads Board has smoothed out the bumps … fit the 'bus' with a set of lately-invented balloon tyres." (The Newer Cobb and Co., 8 Mar 1924, p.24)

THE TOOWOOMBA CHRONICLE

The Toowoomba Chronicle. "the leading newspaper of the Darling Downs, was started as far back as the year 1861, two years after separation had been granted to Queensland. Its founder was Mr. Darius Hunt, of Parramatta, who was invited to Toowoomba to establish a newspaper by those who were actuated principally by a desire to oppose the then existing paper, which was a strong advocate of the old conservative school of squatters. Mr. W. H. Groom, the present proprietor, joined Mr. Hunt in 1874 as partner, and assumed the editorship of the Chronicle.

In 1877 he purchased Mr. Hunt's share, and since then the paper has remained in the undisturbed possession of the Groom family. In 1874 the Liberal party, with Mr. Macalister at the head, came into power, and the Chronicle supported that party, and, indeed, has stuck to Liberal principles ever since. The essence of the policy of the Chronicle may be described as 'close settlement on the lands' and no paper in Queensland has more tenaciously clung to the principle which called it into existence ; and it has been rewarded with a great measure of success, for thousands of small farmers are now settled on the Downs lands, and are readers of the Chronicle. It has always been Liberal in politics, and strongly, with no uncertain tone, advocated those principles which it believed to be necessary for the advancement of the people. As a consequence, the Chronicle commands considerable influence on the Downs, and for 33 years its proprietor has been returned to Parliament as representative for the town of Toowoomba, and for five years he occupied the distinguished position of Speaker of the Queensland Legislative Assembly ... The paper is printed on a double-royal machine, one of the latest design, and on Saturdays it is compelled to stretch itself out to eight, and not infrequently runs to 10 pages. It is handsomely supported by advertisers, probably in a greater degree than any other provincial newspaper in the colony. The premises occupied by the Chronicle are neat, and internally very commodious, and everything that is necessary to the production of a great newspaper can be found within the four walls of the Chronicle office." (The Toowoomba Chronicle, 17 Nov 1894, p.1016)

DOWNS CO-OPERATIVE BUTTER FACTORY

ca. 1908 Toowoomba "holds pride of place in point of seniority and success ... It demonstrates what grit, determination, and concerted effort, directed on sound lines, can achieve. And to-day, the company is a signal example of the old adage, 'From what a small seed a giant oak may spring.' ... From Westbrook ... advisableness of forming a butter and bacon company, with a factory on the railway near Toowoomba ... By deciding on Toowoomba, the converging point of the Downs railways, as a site, the proposed company had a chance of being—what it has since become—a powerful Downs business, drawing its supplies from districts served by two main and three branch railway lines ... Promises of support were received from Nobby, Clifton, Clifton Back Plains, Allora, Southbrook, Gowrie Junction, Glencoe, and Highfields ... good site ... new machinery ... best manager ... Messers. Purcell, McAlpine, Irvine, Handley, Read, Banks, and Canon Pughe ... first permanent directors." (The History of Queensland, 1923, p.609)

Coach & mail conveyance

1866 – COMPLAINTS "The contracts of the firm Cobb and Co. by coach, which now include ... Toowoomba to Warwick, have been carried out with the greatest regularity." (Coaching in Australia, W. Lees, 1917, p.49) While "(From the D. D. Gazette.) Cobb and Co's Coaches.— Great complaints are prevalent in this town concerning the manner in which Cobb and Co. are performing their mail contract. The mails have frequently been delivered long beyond the contract time, and this is inexcusable when we find the coaches coming up overloaded with passengers—in fact, uncomfortably crowded. The fact is, that if Messrs. Cobb and Co. lay themselves out for passenger traffic, they should make arrangements so that this traffic for the benefit of the contractors should not interfere with the due delivery of her Majesty's mails in Toowoomba." (Toowoomba and Drayton, 1 May 1866, p.3)

"COBB AND CO'S COACHES. For Ipswich and Toowoomba, daily at 6.25 a.m. and at noon. For Dalby, Wednesdays, Fridays, and Saturdays ... The new railway time-table which is to be in force to-morrow when the line is to be opened for regular traffic to Gatton, will make considerable difference in the coaching arrangements, and it is desirable that travellers should be clearly informed of them ... The journey down, from Toowoomba to Brisbane, is thus to be performed in ten hours or less—the up journey occupying eleven hours. By this new arrangement, a person may leave Toowoomba in the morning, and, after spending more than four hours in Ipswich, reach home again before midnight.—Q. Times, y 31." (Cobb and Co's Coaches, 2 Jun 1866, p.4) See *Appendix 5.1 Mail Routes 1864*

1867 – "THE MAIL SERVICE. The following is a statement which we have obtained through the courtesy of the postal authorities, showing the names of the successful tenderers for the performance of the mail service for 1868-69." (The Mail Service, 26 Oct 1867, p.5) See *Appendix 4.1 Tenders for Mail Service 1868-1869*

"MAIL BETWEEN TOOWOOMBA AND HIGHFIELDS. A copy of the following letter was handed us last evening for publication : — General Post-Office, Brisbane, November 5, 1867. Sir— ... I will shortly call for tenders for a weekly mail service between Toowoomba and Highfields, to commence on the 1st January next, on which date also the Post-office at the latter place will be re-opened, in charge of Mr. J. W. De Gruchey ... Thomas L. Murray Prior, Postmaster-General. W. H. Groom, Esquire." (Mail between Toowoomba and Highfields, 9 Nov 1867, p.2)

1881 – SWAGMAN ROBBED TOOWOOMBA MAIL "It appears ... the mailman was on his way down to Dalby from Goondiwindi, he met a swag-man on the road ... the swagman seized hold of the rein of the pack-horse, drew a six- chambered revolver ... the robber then proceeded to put his own swag on the horse carrying the mail ... mounted the other, and rode away into the bush ... it is sincerely to be hoped that this bushranger may soon be brought to justice." (Robbery of the Toowoomba Mail, 18 Jan 1881, p.3)

1901 – "TOOWOOMBA AND DRAYTON. Mail Route.— Distance, 4 Miles. Toowoomba and Charleville. Railway. Mail Route. Toowoomba to Gowrie Junction, 8 miles; thence to Gowrie railway station, 4; Oakey Creek railway station, 6; Jondaryan railway station, 9; Bowenville, 8; Blaxland's Siding, 13; Dalby, 3; Macalister, 15; Warra, 13; Chinchilla, 22; Miles, 28; Paddy's Creek, 4; Dulacca, 22; Channing's, 14; Yeulba, 9; Blythedale, 7; Roma, 20; Bungeworgorai, 16; Hodson, 6; Brinsop, 9; Muckadilla, 6; Amby, 12; East Mitchell, 14; Mitchell, 1; Womallala, 10; Mugallala, 19; Dulbydilla, 10; Morven, 16; Augathella, 15; Charleville, 42. Total, 382 miles. (Pugh's Queensland almanac and directory, 1901)

Buckboard buggy, hired from Cobb and Co.
(Walter and Katie Hume Collection) – The University of Queensland

1932 Old porch at the Royal Bull's Head Inn,
Drayton – Courtesy State Library of Queensland

1924 One of the original old homes of Drayton; now
the post office, was Bull's Head Hotel (C. W. Callaghan)
– The Brisbane Courier, 30 Jun 1924, p.10

1932 Royal Bull's Head Inn, 1879; late 1890s private residence,
named `The Terrace'; 1890s-1952 housed the Drayton
Post Office – Courtesy State Library of Queensland

ca. 1882 Panoramic view of Toowoomba – Courtesy State Library of Queensland

The Toowoomba Chronicle, 17 Nov 1894 – Courtesy National Library of Australia

ca. 1856 Meehan's Hotel in Darling Street, Drayton – Courtesy State Library of Queensland

View of Herries Street, Toowoomba (Sir J. R. Kemp) – Courtesy State Library of Queensland

ca. 1881 Ruthven Street, Toowoomba (L. E. Polak) – Courtesy State Library of Queensland

1910-1911 Ruthven Street, Toowoomba (Taylor Series) – Courtesy State Library of Queensland

1910-1911 Ruthven Street, Toowoomba (Taylor Series) – Courtesy State Library of Queensland

Toowoomba's first post office was built during 1864/65 and opened in September 1865 on the corner of Ruthven and Russel Streets, while in 1878/79 a new post office was erected in Margaret Street – Courtesy State Library of Queensland

10th December 1884 Group pictured on verandah at Euston Homestead,
Drayton (Hume Family Collection) – Courtesy The University of Queensland

ca. 1870 Office at Fountain's Camp outside Toowoomba – Courtesy State Library of Queensland

1877 `The Hermitage' second home of Walter and Katie Hume, Toowoomba (Hume Family Collection) – Courtesy The University of Queensland

1889 Fairholme residence at Toowoomba – Courtesy State Library of Queensland

North Toowoomba Boy's School – Courtesy State Library of Queensland

ca. 1870 View of Westbrook Station on the Darling Downs, south of Toowoomba – Courtesy State Library of Queensland

ca. 1908 Downs Co-operative Butter Factory, Toowoomba, The History of Queensland, 1923, p.609

ca. 1889 Crowd in Ruthven Street, Toowoomba – Courtesy State Library of Queensland

Chapter Five

The western mail run

NORTHWARD TO THE SHED.
By W. Ogilvie

From the green bends of the Murray they have run their horses in,
For there's haste and there is hurry when the Queensland sheds begin.
On the Bogan they are bridling, they are saddling on the Bland,
There is plunging and there's sidling—for the colts don't understand
That the Western creeks are calling,
And the idle days are done
With the snowy fleeces falling
And the Queensland sheds begun.

Hark the music of the battle! it is time to bare our swords:
Do you hear the rush and rattle as they tramp along the boards?
They are past the pen-doors picking light-woolled weaners one by one;
I can hear the shear-blades clicking, and I know the fight's begun !

(Northward to the Shed, Verses 1&3, 27 Apr 1901, p.7)

Mail conveyance to the west

1859 – QUEENSLAND "Conveyance of Mails. Tenders are required by the Postmaster General for the conveyance of mails for one or three years from 1st January next. Tenders to be sent in on or before 12 o'clock on Wednesday, October 19th … The following services have reference to Queensland. 1. From and to Tenterfield and Frazer's Creek, once a week; 2. From and to Casino and the Richmond River Heads, once a week; 3. From and to Casino and Brisbane, once a week; 4. From and to Ipswich and Brisbane, daily; 5. From and to Timbarra Gold Diggings (Tableland) and Tenterfield, trice a week; 6. From and to Drayton and Calandoon, via Canal Creek, once a week; 7. From and to Drayton and Dalby, once a week; 6. From and to Dalby and Condamine, via Daandine, Warra Warra, and Wambo, once a week; 9. From and to Condamine and Surat, once a week; 10. From and to Condamine and Taroon on the Dawson River via Wallann and Juandah, once a week." (Conveyance of Mails, 27 Sep 1859, p.3)

1869 – "CONVEYANCE OF MAILS FOR 1870 Amongst the list of accepted tenders for the conveyance of mails for 1870 … William Wallis, Goondiwindi, 48; Condamine and Surat, via Undullah, Murrilla, Warkon, Bingie, and Nooriudee; once a week; horse; two years: £149 per annum … Cobb and Co., Brisbane, 18; Dalby and Condamine, via Kogan and Wombo; twice a week; coach; two years. Cobb and Co., Brisbane, 14; Condamine and Roma via Morabie, Wallumbilla, and Blythedale; twice a week; coach; two years. Cobb and Co., Brisbane, 44; Warwick, Maryland (N.S.W.); and Tenterfield (N.S.W.) twice a week; coach; two year … Total amount of tenders accepted from Cobb and Co., £5058 19s 8d per annum" (Conseyance of Mails for 1870, 11 Dec 1869, p.2) See *Appendix 2.5 1863 Map of Queensland, showing road between Drayton, Dalby, Condamine and Surat*

First Stage—Drayton to Dalby

1864 – POSTAL ARRANGEMENTS ALTERATIONS "We shall have a twice a week conveyance, irrespective of the mail, between Dalby and Toowoomba at the beginning of the new year. And we trust thereby to effect some alteration in the present aboard postal arrangements. Dalby, 20th December, 1864." (Dalby, 24 Dec 1864, p.3)

1870 – WASHING TUB PROVING ABORTIVE "DALBY. As we predicted in our last issue, the late rains caused floods, and the floods have done considerable damage to the roads … There has, of course, been an interruption to the communication with the up-country districts during the week, and a consequent detention of mails … all attempts made by Cobb and Co.'s agents to transport them across the creek there by means of ropes and a washing-tub proving abortive." (Dalby, 3 Dec 1870, p.10)

1890 – DALBY "On the Darling Downs and Myall creek, electorate of Dalby … with money-order office, savings bank, and telegraph station, and station on the Western Railway, about 140 miles by road W. of Brisbane (152 miles by rail), and 130 miles distant from Ipswich. The Royal, Post Office, Queen's Arms, and Golden Fleece are the leading hotels … A weekly coach runs to St. George … Hares are now plentiful on Jimbour station … Population of district 1,317 (census 1886). The Dalby Herald is the local paper." (The Australian Handbook, 1890)

Second Stage—Dalby to Condamine

1865 – INCREASED TRAFFIC "Owing to the increased passenger traffic between here and Condamine, the mail contractor started four-horse conveyance, seated to carry eight passengers. Evident care has been taken in its construction to give comfort to the passengers and from the appearance of the horses, it is to be expected that no delay will be caused through knocking up, as was the case last winter." (Dalby, 27 Mar 1865, p.3)

1865 – MAIL STUCK UP "On Friday last came information of the Condamine and Taroom mail being again stuck up

—this time by two men, with their faces covered with sheepskin masks—

the last mentioned robbery making the third mail robbery within three weeks. Any person who is familiar with the tactics of bushrangers must be aware that delay and indiscreet communicativeness must prelude the probability of the police being successful." (Roma, 5 Dec 1865, p.4)

1867 – DELAYED LETTERS "Numerous parties in Condamine have had letters delayed and sent all over the colony before getting them. Surely, if a letter is directed to Condamine, there is no necessity for its making the 'grand tour' before its reaching its destination." (Condamine, 2 Nov 1867, p.3)

1873 – COBB'S INDIFFERENCE "Condamine … Not much change in either wind or weather. By the bye, the latter is rather damp, at all events there has been heavy fogs, which is fully demonstrated by the fact that our mail communication, which is supplied by Cobb and Co's coach, usually gets here the day after it is due. At one time Cobb's arrival and departure was as perfect as clockwork, but now seems to be laboring under a state of happy indifference or chronic delays. What would A. Trollope say if he travelled by Cobb on the Dalby and Roma road? … A very fine lot of fat cattle—200 head—passed here on the 1st from Northampton Downs, for delivery to one of the Brisbane butchers. I am informed that delivery is to be taken at Jondaryan, the price is £7 for bullocks and £6 for cows." (Condamine, 9 Apr 1873, p.3)

Third Stage—Condamine to Surat

1867 – BIG BINGY'S HEROISM "Surat … the river Ballone still heads in the same direction. I was pained to witness a most distressing scene in the bed of this well-known stream … A respected Suratter managed to get stuck, dray, bag and baggage, in the treacherous depths of the river.

Horse flesh could do no more ... an act of manly heroism on the part of our old friend Big Bingy, which really deserves recording ... a plunge in the water, and ere the miserable quadruped in the shafts had time to cock his ears, and give a snort, he was wrenched out of his harness, and his place filled by the Big 'un. An appalling yell, apparently from under his tail, startled the leader into activity, and up the bank they went, as if the ponderous dray had been only a wheelbarrow ... An unfortunate horse was left in a deplorable state, and all from catching a glimps of his driver. The said Jehu had mounted a terrific hat a la Cobb and Co. And I may remark here that these hats have a charmed reputation. The moment a Roman mounts one, his character as a 'whip' is established. In an evil moment the man in the hat left his perch,

and dismounted for the purpose of blowing his nose. (His own, not the horse's).

The poor animal evidently took him for something supernatural, and was seized with gripes of so enduring a character, that he was abandoned to the crows and dingoes. A fabulous price has since been offered for the hat, under the impression that no jibber could stand it." While "in the main street of Surat (there's only one, so it is hard to miss) ... a brazen flourish from the trumpets ... for the Jackeroo Ball ... picnic followed the next day ... you will be glad to hear the Roma Butcher has resumed business again, and Mr. Burgess, from Surat, has opened a shop in McDowall-street ... Mr. Merry's goods have arrived at last, and his store opens on the 30th. I found flour just double the price in Surat, and sugar much higher than in Roma ... One short fall of rain did some good, but was succeeded by a cold drying wind that went as far towards withering up the grass as the hottest sun could have done. Lambing pronounced to be the best known for years." (Roma, 5 Oct 1867, p.3)

1890 – CONDAMINE "The larger cities have come to stay ... already pushing their way well into the suburbs and over the dotted line into the next parish. Distance seems no obstacle, nor for that matter do roads ... Hotel: Condamine Arms ... The communication with the metropolis is via the Miles railway ... Population, 83 (census 1886)." (The Australian Handbook, 1890)

1890 – COBB'S COACHES AT SURAT "a post-town, with money-order, savings bank, and telegraph office, in the country of Elgin, electorate of Murilla, police district of Surat, situated on the Balonne river, about 50 miles (61 postal) SE. of Roma, 84 from St George, and 346 miles (by rail and coach route) due W. of Brisbane. Cobb's coaches run twice a week from Yeulba Railway Station through Surat on to St George ... a bridge spans the Balonne at this point ... Population 188 (census 1886)." (The Australian Handbook, 1890)

1917 – SURAT PEOPLE HOSPITABLE AND OPEN-HEARTED "Surat surprises a visitor who remembers that its history dates from the earliest days. One drives through a town, small and scattered certainly, but looking as new and fresh as paint could make it, and as I saw it in early evening, when the sun shone from over the Western hills, the town looked charming ... And charming people I found there, hospitable and open-hearted, a reflex of the splendid lands, which continue from Dogwood Creek down the Balonne, and out to the head waters of the Coogoon, and the far-away Maranoa range. The town is on the left bank of the Balonne, 47miles S.S.W. of Yeulba, and 50 miles S.S.E. of Roma, set on a red soil ridge overlooking the river. It is a neat set-up town with two hotels, the two-storied one I stayed at, the Royal, kept by Mr. C. Simpson, is a charming place in every way; a branch of the Commercial Bank of Sydney, a large State school, School of Arts, Church of England, and R.C. Church, hospital, Post and Telegraph Office, Warroo Shire Council, and ball, and several clubs. The business section covers every trade and profession required in a pastoral centre, and there are well-stocked stores. The chief pastoral holdings are Noorindoo to the east, owned by N. N. Danger and managed by F. R. Rouse; Werribone, to the South, and Glenairn, but large areas have been resumed and quickly selected." (Coaching in Australia, 1917, p.69)

1917 – LEAVING FROM SURAT POST OFFICE "Behind seven horses ... we drove from the Surat Post Office ... across the wooded bridge which spans the deep soil banks of the Balonne ... On Beringa dry creek we pass the site of old Beringa township, a record of misplaced confidence in the future, for the holders of the adjacent blocks were perished out in the big drought of 1901-2 ... belar scrub ... she-oak and black soil flats ... Bainbilla change house ... then comes the prickly pear, which stays with us to Yeulba ... Guppy's Creek ... a pretty stream ... the remnants of a school and Cobb and Co.'s old change house ... we come to one of the best change houses on the Queensland roads, Waldegrave's, where a charming lunch is served ... sand and low ridge ... Blythedale Braystone, one of the chief intake areas of the artesian waters of Queensland ... Generally, however, the coach pulls to a near-by tree, where a, box or tin is nailed, coach-seat high, and, taking out the mail matter and putting other packages or letters in ... Rising a steep ridge ... drove into the station yard at Yeulba, as the West-going train arrived. Yeulba is a small township stretching mainly along the Southern side of the S. and W. line, 281 miles west of Brisbane, with several hotels and stores, the one of chief interest being Messrs. Cobb and Co.'s, where also passengers are booked for Surat and St. George." (Coaching in Australia, 1917, p.69)

The western mail run altered—Dalby, Condamine, Yuleba, Roma, Mitchell and Charleville

YULEBA

1879 – RAILWAY OPENS "Oct. 20.— Western Railway opened to Yeulbah." (Queensland's Half Century 1859 to 1909 Notable Events, 8 Dec 1909, pp.23-37) See *Appendix 1 Map of Queensland - Cobb's Coach Guide*

1890 – POST TOWN "sometimes written as Yuleba, Yuelba, and Yulebah, is a post-town, with savings bank and money- order office, telegraph and railway station on the Western Line, 281 miles W. from Brisbane.

Coaches run to Surat (25s) and St. George (60s) ... The stations in the neighbourhood are Bendemere ... Moongool ... Wallumbilla ... Hotels : Royal, Royal Mail, and Commercial ; billiard saloon ... On the creek of the same name. As this is expected to be the point to which the traffic from Surat, St. George and Cunnamulla will converge, and the depot from which stock will be forwarded by rail, the necessary stock yards and other conveniences have been erected ... Population 158 (census 1886)." (The Australian Handbook, 1890)

1909 – COBB AND CO.'S 'KING OF THE ROAD' reputation shattered "Yeulba Mail Service. The manner in which the St. George-Yeulba mail service is now conducted by Cobb and Co. is very adversely commented on, as on the slightest provocation in the way of bad weather conditions there is a delay in the mail delivery which disorganises the whole outgoing service.

There was a time when Cobb and Co. was regarded as being 'King of the roads' in the matter of doing almost impossibilities in the way of delivering mails and carrying passengers through to time,

but that reputation has been completely shattered by the manner in which the Yeulba to St. George service is now carried on." (Yeulba Mail Service, 25 Aug 1909, p.3)

MITCHELL

1890 – TOWN HAS NOT IMPROVED "A post-town, with money-order office, and telegraph station, and Government Savings Bank, in the county of Dublin, electorate of Maranoa, on the Maranoa river, 371 miles NW. of Brisbane, and 53 miles W. of Roma ... There are six hotels—Post Office and Green Gate being the principal ... a saddler ... two aerated water factories ... The town has not improved, as it was expected it would with the opening of the railway ... A jockey club (Mitchell Downs) is here, and in the neighbourhood is a good race-course ... it was for some little time the terminus of the Western Line, which is now extended to Charleville. Coaches ply to St. George and also to Bolton ... Population 433 (census 1886)." (The Australian Handbook, 1890)

1907 – A SHEEP-SHEARING STORY The following letter to the editor appears in the London Daily Mail: Sir, As an unraveller of all kinds of problems, can you obtain for me proof of the following, given to me by eye-witnesses of the extraordinary records? It is said that one Jack Howe, the Queensland ringer-shearer, some fifteen years ago sheared over 200 sheep per day; also that, before Mr. Richard Lane of Lane's Hotel, Blackall, and Mr. Charles Gray, manager of Alice Downs sheep station, he sheared a sheep in seventeen seconds. On learning that he had been timed, Howe asked to be given another chance of breaking this record. He succeeded in repeating the performance over a full-woolled sheep, doing the catching, etc., in the marvellous time of fourteen seconds. If those who witnessed the event are still alive, might I ask them to communicate their experience to you for publication? Yours faithfully, Ubique 409 Kennedy Street, Winnipeg, Canada

1917 – COBB'S COACHES LEAVE THE NEAT TOWN "Mitchell, 368 miles West of Brisbane, lies a short distance from the line, not far from the Maranoa River, which, at times miles wide, is at others a string of deep holes where fish abound. It is a neat town with good hotels, the Post Office and the Hotel Richards can be well mentioned, and large stores. It is the centre of fine pastoral lands, and a considerable area of wheat is also here. Cobb's coaches leave here at regular intervals." (Coaching in Australia, 1917, p.75)

1889 – WEATHER "On Saturday a most decided change set in ... our nervous system received a shock, by the appearance of a telegram outside the local Post Office, which informed us that we could expect stormy weather." (The Mitchell, 17 Aug 1889, p.29)

1926 – "MITCHELL CHILDREN'S BALL. One of the most successful children's fancy dress balls ever held in Mitchell took place on Thursday night, July 2, under the auspices of the Band candidate in the Most Popular Boy competition." (Mitchell Children's Ball, 7 Jul 1926, p.22)

1902 – MAIL SUSPENSION "May 12.— Suspension until May 16 of carriage of mails in the West by Cobb and Co." (Queensland's Half Century 1859 to 1909 Notable Events, 8 Dec 1909, p.23-37)

1917 – "THE PRESENT DAY COACHING ROUTES of Cobb and Co. (Coaching in Australia, 1917, p.53) See *Appendix 1 Map of Queensland - Cobb's Coach Guide* & *Appendix 6.1 Mail Services*

1923 – PROFIT "For the year to June 30 Cobb and Co., Ltd, reports a net profit £3011, after providing for depreciation. The directors consider this very satisfactory, as the profit was entirely from commercial transactions, no profits this year being made on land or plant, and the conditions generally being adverse for securing good turn-overs. The report continues: The stores returned a profit of £6010, being an increase on last year's figures of £553. The indenting of goods direct also enabled the head office to show a further £499 profit, which is expected to be further increased each year, as the volume of goods indented increases ...

The once great pioneering organisation of the eastern portion of Australia has now only one line of coaches, that from Yeulba to Thallon. Horses, cost a fortune to feed at present, are still being used on the Yeulba to Surat road but from Surat to Thallon motor transport is utilised. Not so long ago the firm had their own coach works in Charleville, and the paysheet for there alone would be bigger than that of the whole organisation to-day.

Coach works and coaches have disappeared with the advent of the motor-car,

and to-day the firm's principal activities centre in supplying all requirements to pastoralists and others in the bush." (Cobb and Co., 20 Oct 1923, p.4)

1868 View of Cunningham Street in Dalby – Courtesy State Library of Queensland

Last bark hut in Dalby, demolished 1940s – Courtesy State Library of Queensland

ca. 1915 Townspeople of Dalby gathering around the Bell Memorial at a recruitment rally – Courtesy State Library of Queensland

ca. 1890 Walter Cunningham Hume, Buggy, a buckboard, "I travelled 1500 miles … Cobb and Co. contracted for the journey, price 200 pounds" (Walter and Katie Hume Collection) – Courtesy The University of Queensland

ca. 1915 Post office and clock tower in Cunningham Street, Dalby, `The dry atmosphere of the Western Downs is most beneficial to all respiratory troubles' – Courtesy State Library of Queensland

ca. 1877 Surat Police Quarters – Courtesy State Library of Queensland

1905 New homestead at Noorindoo Station Surat district – Courtesy State Library of Queensland

Interior of Noorindoo shearing shed – Courtesy State Library of Queensland

1875 Condamine Plains Station Buildings – Courtesy State Library of Queensland

ca. 1875 Stable at Condamine Plains Station – Courtesy State Library of Queensland

ca. 1916 Change house at Waldegrave's along the Yulebah to Surat Cobb & Co. coach route
– Courtesy State Library of Queensland

ca. 1922 Cobb & Co. coach in front of the Yuleba store – Courtesy State Library of Queensland

ca. 1910 Workers outside wheelwright C. Witty's shop in Yuleba – Courtesy State Library of Queensland

ca. 1895 Wheelwrights standing outside C. Witty's wheelwright shop in Yuleba – Courtesy State Library of Queensland

ca. 1913 Signed Yeulba Railway Station – Courtesy State Library of Queensland

ca. 1910 Schoolchildren at the Yuleba State School, Miss Clarinda Moore teacher – Courtesy State Library of Queensland

ca. 1920s View of Yuleba – Courtesy State Library of Queensland

ca. 1915 Recruiting train at Wallumbilla Railway Station – Courtesy State Library of Queensland

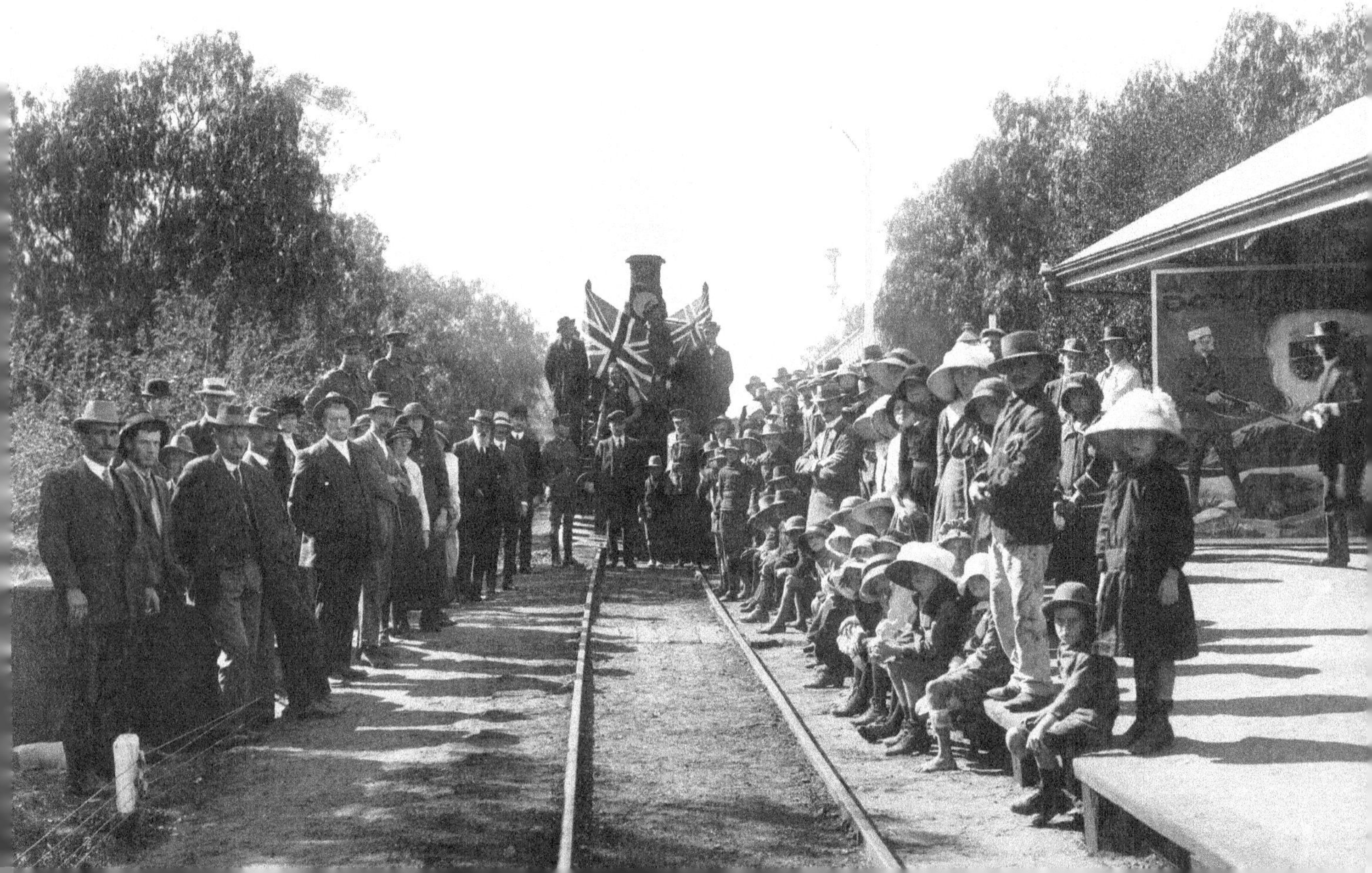

1914 Cobb & Co. coach crossing the swollen Balonne River, Surat – Courtesy State Library of Queensland

1917 Harvesting wheat at Woodside Station, near Roma (Thomas James Murray and his three children, Thomas Welson, Norman James and Agnes) – Courtesy State Library of Queensland

1898 Bullock team with a wool wagon at the Railway Station in Mitchell – Courtesy State Library of Queensland

Harvesting at Hogan's Farm, Mitchell district – Courtesy State Library of Queensland

Early 1900s Post and Telegraph Office in Mitchell – Courtesy Flickr

Railway Station, Mitchell – Courtesy State Library of Queensland

Chapter Six

Roma-a longer stop

THE DROUGHT-SRICKEN AREA.
by Skipper

So destiny has brought us To a far-back western town,
Where one and all their sorrows In 'booze' attempt to drown ;
Where the air is hot and dusty, And humans, too, turn 'rusty',
  Where drought prevails, And nature wears a frown.

We see the mirage glitter Far across the dazzling plain,
And wonder with the squatter, Will it ever rain again?
The caresses of fallen beasts Offend our sense of smell.
  In fact, 'out back' at present Is little short of hell!

The flies are here in hundreds, Red spiders too galore.
And centipedes (we vouch for this) Their sting is mighty sore.
Let's mention too the homely goats, Which wander free as air,
  Their 'butting-in' propensities Just drive us to despair.

Will we ever get a move on From this far back western town?
Will we ever find a grassy spot Where we may settle down?
Through the glare our fancy takes us To a 'garden land' afar,
  Where every tree of Nature grows, Except the Coolibah!

(Original Verse, 11 Jul 1927, p.6)

Early Roma intelligence

In 1867, Roma was quiet. A local writer shared, "Last week I enclosed you a programme of the races, and an account of the first day's sport, together with whatever little news our dullest of townships afforded. This, however, you were destined never to receive, for in order to give the latest intelligence, I, just shortly before the closing of the Post office, went to the racecourse, leaving my 'swag' outside the place I am living in, and lo! ... On my return I found the whole had vanished, in tenues auras, leaving me nothing but the clothes on my back ...

For the last three weeks we have had a scorching sun, with light pleasant breezes, and now a storm or a little more rain would be beneficial to the grass ... Most of the sheep have returned to their various stations, and washing and shearing are progressing. The Mitchell Downs (E. Morey's and Co.), work is finished, and 'the clip' very satisfactory. Cobb's coaches now run twice a week, leaving Roma on Tuesdays and Thursdays at 10 a.m ... Bungil Creek not run last two years—water bad, still no sickness in town, except a few cases of sandy blight.

Cobb and Co. commenced running mail coaches; only two days from Roma to Condamine.

Arrangements are about being made to run through to Dalby in three days." (Roma, 15 Jan 1867, p.3)

By October there was a labour shortage as washing and shearing has commenced on several stations. "Some drays laden with the first clip had passed through the town, I had hoped to have sent in my present communication an account of a little more life in the township and brisker transactions in business affairs. I am sorry I am unable to do so. Two things prevent this ... a scarcity of labour ... and the rush which has taken place to the diggings. William Cole, better known as 'scrammy Bill,' has been sent to gaol for twelve months, for 'soldiering' one of Cobb and Co.'s horses. The police have had their eyes upon him for some time past." (Roma, 31 Oct 1867, p.4)

In 1869, change came. "The Minister for Works, Arthur Macalister, visited. He came with others in a Cobb and Co. coach and stayed at Mr. John Cook's Hotel. They talked about ... many matters affecting the present and future welfare of the town ... particularly those relating to the expenditure of money voted for street expenditure, Post and Telegraph Offices, &c., &c ... On Thursday morning ... drove and rode out to inspect the site of the proposed bridge, at Bungeworgorai ... On Friday evening Mr. Macalister attended a banquet to which he had been invited by the principal inhabitants of Roma. About thirty-five gentlemen sat down to dinner in the billiard-room of Mr. Chas. Ahrens, at the Club-house ... a discussion on various subjects ensued, amongst the most prominent of which was the railway question." (Roma, 23 Oct 1869, p.10)

In 1870, things looked better. "The weather since my last has been everything that could be desired. Cobb and Co. arrived yesterday at the usual time, and bullock and horse drays, are again able to move ... Potatoes from Toowoomba at 18s. per hundred pounds, delivered at the door, and good winter crops we anticipated by the market gardeners of Roma ...

Are you in secrets of Cabinet Ministers ? If you are, give me a hint as to when Roma and Dalby railway extension bill is likely to be brought in. I want to buy an allotment or two near the place where I think the station will be." (Roma, 30 Mar 1870, p.3)

"An incident of rather an amusing character took place a few days since. A young couple recently committed matrimony, and went into the service of an hotel-keeper in the town. Matters passed on smoothly enough, until one day in the latter part of last week, when, mirabile dictan! who should walk into the hotel and order dinner but the 'first' husband of the 'ladie fayre.' He was supposed to have been gathered to his father's years ago. It reminds one of Byron's 'Beppo.' It is gratifying, however, to know that no 'scene' occurred, benedict No 1 cheerfully conceding his pre-emptive right to benedict No 2; and benedict No 1, like the Man in Scripture when relieved by the good Samaritan, went on his way rejoicing ...

The contractors for the various Municipal improvements are pushing their work with great activity. The metalling of McDowall-street, forming side paths, water-tables, &c., are rapidly being proceed with, and we confidently anticipate before another flood occurs being able to make our way through the principal thoroughfare of the town with tolerable ease and comfort." (Roma, 30 Mar 1870, p.3)

Drought hit hard in 1874 "Sept. 28. — Serious drought in the West ; carriers at Roma refused to accept loading." (Queensland's Half Century 1859 to 1909 Notable Events, 8 Dec 1909, pp.23-37)

Five years later a coal survey brought hope. "Coal Between Dalby and Roma ... In accordance with your instruction to examine the country along the line of railway from Dalby, with a view of ascertaining the existence, or otherwise, of coal available for the use of the line, I have now the honour to report that I proceeded to Roma, and examined the country, for ten miles each side of the Railway line from Channing to Hodgson ... From the town site of Miles to Blyth's Creek, the formation consists of an upper coarse, sandstone of irregular texture ... On the west side of Yuleba Creek, on the north side of the railway ... it was ascertained that at least 50 feet of brown shale and about the same thickness of coarse sandstone ... Approaching Roma, the upper part of the brown shale contains thin beds of limestone, with many fossil shells and corals, also belemnites ; the whole indicating a marine deposit of the cretaceous period, while thin flakes of gypsum also point to a saltwater origin ... To the west of Blyth's Creek, the eretaceous shales and limestone are most extensively developed, and approaching Mount Abundance the country gradually improves ... Between Blyth's Creek and Bungil Creek ... there is an outburst of basalt, which forms the Grafton Range ...

On the west side of Grafton Range, in the bed of the Bungil Creek at the upper boundary of Roma Town Common, the carboniferous sandstones are exposed … In Bungeworgorai Creek, about ten miles above the main Western road … many good specimens of ferns were found … A good seam of coal is reported to have been found about twenty miles higher up the creek near the Dividing Range … In 1885 … forty miles beyond Dalby … there are several thin seams of good cannel coal … coal is hard gas coal, which does not cake … it burns very quickly … it requires some special experience in the firing of locomotives" (Coal between Dalby and Roma, 25 Oct 1879, p.4) And then the railway finally reached Roma: "Sept. 16.— Railway to Roma opened. Nov. 1.— Postal cards first issued in Queensland." (Queensland's Half Century 1859 to 1909 Notable Events, 8 Dec 1909, pp.23-37)

In 1884, drought returned. "From Toowoomba to Roma, which was until recently the terminus of the S. and W. railway, the line traverses the northern portion of the famous Darling Downs, called by the people of the north the 'Garden of Queensland' … the most severe drought known for years in that part of the country. From the carriage window were seen at intervals sheep and cattle dying by the hundred, not for want of drinking water, of which there was a sufficient supply, but owing to the need of grass and rain to moisten the parched earth. You can easily imagine this state of things made the inhabitants wear grave countenances, and while mingling with them I used their faces as my barometer. Happily the dry weather seems to have broken up, and rain has of late been falling to some extent in these suffering localities."

In that same report Roma with described with a dry wit: "At a place called Miles we stopped for dinner … Roma was reached at 10.30 p.m., and, as I was informed, a hotel bearing the royal cognomen of the Queen's Arms was the best, I drove up in their conveyance and was accommodated with a 'shakedown,' the beds all being bespoke.

I also became acquainted with the cockroaches which inhabit this locality. They are not as large as those in Brisbane, where I have mistaken them for mice, but they are more numerous and, I think, more intelligent, for on one occasion I saw them playing on the piano.

Roma may most appropriately be called a 'wooden town.' I do not remember seeing a brick or stone structure about it. On the outskirts may be seen houses built on a style of architecture now discarded in town, the building material chiefly used consisting of logs, bark, and old tin." (Roma, Queensland, 5 Jan 1884, p.26)

While McDowall Street showed how much Roma had changed. "Since the advent of the railway Roma has made great advancement in population and appearance. The former are computed at 2000. The streets are broad, and the roadways in a very fair state. McDowall-street is the main thoroughfare. I was told by a townsman that five years ago you would not have recognised it as the same, so much had it grown and changed in appearance for the better … The post and telegraph offices are situated in this street, and during the delivery of the mail each morning it assumes its busiest and most lively appearance. Next to the post office is the town hall, which resembles a toy bank, on a large scale, with the paint rubbed off. This latter defect seems to prevail universally throughout the town, whether for lack of a painter or antipathy to the article itself I do not know. A little farther along the street on the same side as the town hall the conspicuous sign of L. Tolano, tobacconist, catches the eye, and if the observer be a consumer of the weed, he could not do better than give Mr. Tolano a call, as he has that article in all its varieties. And he has a large assortment of books, stationery, and fancy goods, and is also the agent for the 'Town and Country Journal' and other leading papers.

Although only established about a year, the business has grown rapidly, necessitating the enlargement of the shop, the better to accommodate an addition, in the shape of a watchmaking and jewellery department, so that one can safely say that at present it is the leading business of its kind in the town. Not content with this, Mr. Tolano, who is energetic and enterprising, has lately opened a branch at Mitchell, now the terminus of the railway. On the opposite side of the street are the premises of J. Lister, well stocked with ironmongery, furniture, guns, and tinware. As plumber, iron worker, and tinsmith, Mr. Lister's business ranks second to none in the whole western district. He manufactures everything in the trade, but makes a specialty of travelling trunks (which are preferred by those who use them to the English make), and tanks which have been made and set up on stations, say within a radius of 150 miles. Mr. Lister opened the business in June, 1875, since which time both the business and the town have made rapid strides, but I think the race so far has been fairly won by the former … Roma depends on the large stations by which it is surrounded, and to which it is the outlet. As the season had proved very bad, owing to the drought, business was rather dull. Had it been the reverse, I do not think it would have made any material difference in the quiet appearance of the street, although it might have put more paint on the houses." (Roma, Queensland, 5 Jan 1884, p.26)

By 1890, Roma "a thriving township on Bungil Creek, in the county of Waldegrave, and electoral district of Maranoa, 318 NW. of Brisbane. It has a repeating telegraph station, savings bank, money-order office and railway station … eleven hotels—among others, School of Arts, Queen's Arms, Royal, and Railway, the first substantial two-storied building … and a brewery … Till October, 1883, it was the terminus of the Western Railway, but the line is now open to Charleville … also a School of Arts with library of 1,067 vols … There are some good gardens, and the vine is extensively and successfully grown, and promises to become an important and profitably industry … The population by census 1886 was 1,727. Newspaper, Western Star." (The Australian Handbook, 1890)

In 1902, Roma had grown even more. "The town of Roma is 318 miles from Brisbane, and 218 from Toowoomba, situated on the Southern and Western Railway. Its population according to the census of 1901, is 2,373 persons ; the population of the district 7,110. The land is unquestionably of first-class character and quality, and is well adapted for grapes and fruit trees of all descriptions, in particular the orange. A large influx of settlers has taken place during the last few years. Many of them have come from South Australia and Victoria, attracted by the glowing reports of the remarkable fertility of the lands in the Maranoa district, for the cultivation of wheat. This cereal is now firmly established, and the staple agricultural industry in the district. With a steadily increasing land settlement, and cultivated areas, the future of the Maranoa as a great agricultural centre is assured, and Roma is already recognised as the central town of South-Western Queensland… The vine flourishes at Roma luxuriantly, and there are several vineyards of over 30 acres in extent, and others varying from 4 to 20 acres each …

Early in 1897 the Municipal Council entered into a contract with the Government to sink an artesian bore in Roma. The terms of agreement were that the Municipality should pay half the cost, and the Government the other half, the boring to be continued until a supply sufficient for the wants of the town had been tapped. In the event of no water supply being obtained the Government were to bear the whole cost of the work. Actual boring was commenced on July 6th, and, after about a month's constant work, a first supply was struck at a depth of 700 ft., the water just rising above the top of the casing. Boring was continued until a supply of 300,000 gallons per day was struck, at a depth of under 1700 ft. This was not considered a sufficient supply by the ratepayers, but, in spite of protests and an offer by the Council to continue boring at its own expense, the Government removed the plant, and shut down the bore. The Council has refused to take over the bore in its present unfinished condition. As the outcome of negotiations with the Government a second bore has been put down near the site of the first one. This second bore is now down about 3700 feet, and the flow from it is 310,000 gallons per day. The flow from the first bore has decreased to 60,000 gallons per day. Early in 1901, a large quantity of natural gas was encountered in the new bore, which at present is allowed to escape by a pipe separate from that by which the water escapes. Tests of the gas show it to be of very high quality as an illuminant, and the Municipal Council has decided to make it available for the use of the ratepayers. The pipes for reticulating the town with water are being delivered, and the work of laying them will be proceeded with immediately. Early last year Mr. Renwick commenced his contract for the erection of a new court house, which is to cost £6000. The work is almost completed, under the supervision of Mr. P. H. Johnson, Government Inspector of Works.

The sum of £6000 has also been voted by Parliament for the erection of a new gaol in Roma, the total cost to be £6000. Roma has a public Hospital, Gaol, State School, Convent School, School of Arts, two Masonic Lodges, Hibernian Benefit Society, Oddfellows' Lodge, Protestant Alliance Society, Good Templars' Lodge, and several other societies, all more or less in a healthy condition."

Roma residents (1902)

"The Mayor of Roma is John N. Bones, Esq., and the Town Clerk is Mr. G. L. Chrystal.
The Parliamentary representative of the district of Maranoa, of which Roma forms a part, is the Hon. Arthur Rutledge, K.C., and Attorney-General.
The Press is represented by the Western Star, published bi-weekly, and Maranoa Advocate, bi-weekly.
Ecclesiastical. Church of England.—Vicar—Rev. Mr. Reiss. Roman Catholic.— Rev. Father P. Capra, Father Lee. Presbyterian.
—Vacant. Wesleyan.—Rev. AV. Faulkner. Church of Christ.—Rev. Mr. Gilmour.
Public Institutions. Roma State School.—Joseph Mayfield, head teacher ; Albert J. Mills, Mary A. C. Rees, Amelia Cowell, W. Zerner, assistant teachers ; George Cook, Ada S. Robinson, Muriel Ida Turnbull, pupil teachers. Total enrolment 401 • daily average attendance, 320. Committee—F. W. E. Faithfull (Chairman), G. L. Chrystal (Secretary), John Rogers, Richard Bryant, W. Miscamble, Carl H. Hoffmann, and W. G. Mayne.
Roma Hospital.—President—James Lalor, M.L.C. ; Vice-Presidents—A. R. McGregor and Seaborne May; Treasurer—F. W. E. Faithfull ; Committee—Messrs J. Rogers, J. N. Bones, E. H. Decker, M. J. Johnston, Lewis Jackson, D. McNaughton, E. F. Craven, G. P. Williams, Joseph Warren, and W. G. Mayne ; Secretary—Phillip Browne; Auditors—H. Catling and E. A. Rees : Wardsman—Skiffington ; Matron—Mrs. E. Turnbull ; Medical Officer—G. S. L'Estrange.
Bungil Divisional Board.—James Lalor, M.L.C. (Chairman), S. May, T. Ferrier, H. McLoughlin, Joseph Lister, G. Williamson ; Secretary and Foreman of Works, &c.—Donald Ross.
LEICRLHARDT Rabbit Board.—A. R. McGregor (Chairman), Hon. J. Lalor, M.LC., J. Richardson, Chas. Flower, R. C. Lethbridge, R. Douglas, F. A. Deshon, A. R. Scott, J. A. Winten; Clerk—R. H. Dyball; Inspector—B. T. Harris.
Boarding School.—R. C. Convent, and 'Highlands,' conducted by Mrs. Murray.
Municipal Council.—J. N. Bones (Mayor), George Ward, S. R. N. Taudevin, T. A. Spencer, R. Conlan, W. B. Murphy, W. Miscamble, John Rogers, C. W. Conroy ; Town Clerk—G. Chrystal; Foreman of Works—S. Wilson ; Town Inspector—W. Lenihan; Auditors—H. O. Catling and A. C. Harvey.
Local Public Officers.—Police Magistrate, Clerk of Petty Sessions, and Returning Officer—E. F. Craven; Assistant C.P.S., Inspector of Factories and Shops and Electoral Registrar.—W. Simpson ; Land

Commissioner—L. Jackson ; Inspector of Slaughter Houses—Francis : Sergeant of Police—Sergeant Small ; eleven constables ; Poundkeeper—E. O'Connor ; Railway Stationmaster—P. Nolan ; District Traffic Manager—J. A. Fraser ; Postmaster and Telegraph Master—H. P. Beech ; Operators—G. Maskel, Bradshaw ; Assistants—T. Townsley, W. Walduck, R. Muir ; Messenger—Reid.

Local Justices of the Peace.—J. Saunders, L. Jackson, T. A. Spencer, J. Lister, J. Lalor, G. S. L'Estrange, F. W. E. Faithfull, S. May, J. Nimmo, J. Wieneke, G. L. Chrystal, D. Ross, W. Harland, S. S. Bassett, Thos. Ferrier, D. McNaughton, G. H. Nind, Geo. Taylor, Paul Volkmann, A. Bollman, J. Warren, H. N. Wilson, A. Cumming, J. G. Dickson (Toomoo), Angus McPherson, W. B. Murphy, U. J. Cunneen, S. R. N. Taudevin, H. H. Barton, M. J. Kelly, John Taylor (Russell Park, Surat), F. B. Bays (Surat), J. M. Hunter (Roma), J. A. Hunter (Yeulba).

Gaol.—Governor—F. Schneider; Matron—Mrs. Schneider; Principal Turnkey—John Murphy ; and 3 Turnkeys.

Cemetery Trustees.—Hon. J. Lalor, M.L.C. (Chairman), W. G. Mayne, J. M. Hunter, Alfred Robinson, Joseph Warren, James Saunders ; E. O'Connor (Secretary).

Societies. Maranoa Lodge, No. 730, S.C.—John Trappett, Secretary. Meets Thursday on or before full moon. Maranoa Royal Arch Chapter, 247, S.C.—John Trappett, Scribe E. Meets third Wednesday in each month.

Raphael Lodge, No. 1850, E.C.—T. D. Wright, Secretary. Meets every second Wednesday in each month.

Raphael Royal Arch Chapter, E.C.—Charles Ladner, Scribe E. Meets fourth Wednesday in February, April, June, August, and October.

Pioneer Lodge, No. 19, P.A.F.S.O.A.—Philip Browne, Secretary. Meets every alternate Monday night.

Hibernian Society.—R. Cunningham, Secretary.

Loyal Western Star Lodge, M.U.1.0.0.F., No. 90.—J. Reid, Secretary. Meets every alternate Tuesday night.

Roma Tennis Club.—Secretary and Treasurer—A. J. Mills.

Western Queensland Racing Club.—President — Hon. J. Lalor ; Vice-President—R. C. Lethbridge ; Secretary—E. O'Connor. Waldegrave Cricket Club.— Secretary—G. Maskel, and P. A. Robinson.

Roma School or Arts Chess and Draughts Club.— Secretary and Treasurer—P. A. Robinson.

Western Queensland Pastoral and Agricultural Association.—President—R. C. Lethbridge; Vice-President—D. McNaughton ; Secretary—Angus McPherson.

School or Arts.—Patron—Hon. J. Lalor, M.L.C. ; President—J. Mayfield ; Secretary and Librarian—Philip Browne ; Treasurer F. W. E. Faithfull.

Roma Amateur Turf Club—Secretary, A. C. Harvey."

Roma Business Directory (1902)

"Wine and Spirit Merchants.—McNaughton and Co. General Storekeepers.—Bryant and McLean, D. McNaughton and Co., W. B. Murphy, Bayard and Co., Hunter and Company, Hoskins and Co.

Wine Makers.—S. S. Bassett, Patrick Smith, M. Barat.

Stationers.—Joseph Warren, J. Saunders, J. Sparks, Grigg and Co., and S. R. N. Taudevin.

Cabinetmakers and Upholsterers.—C. H. Hoffmann, J. Crawford.

Hairdressers.—J. C. Forrester, C. W. Conroy.

Boiling Down Works.—New Zealand Loan and Mercantile Agency Company, Blythdale.

Insurance Agents.—North British Fire Insurance Company—E. H. Decker and Co. ; Imperial Fire Insurance Company—E. H. Decker and Co. ; New Zealand Insurance Company, South British of New Zealand, and National Agency of New Zealand—T. A. Spencer ; Colonial Mutual Life Assurance Society—E. H. Decker and Co. ; Queen Insurance Company (Fire and Life), United Insurance Company, Mutual Life Association of Australasia—J. Saunders.; Mutual of Victoria, and Royal (Fire) —P. Browne ; Commercial Union—J. Saunders ; Colonial Mutual Fire Insurance, London and Lancashire Fire Insurance—G. L. Chrystal; London and Liverpool and Globe, E. O'Connor; British Foreign and Marine Insurance Company, The United Insurance Company, Ltd., Mutual Life Assurance Company of New York—Angus McPherson and Co.

Hotelkeepers.—F. J. Pearse, Royal Hotel; Mrs. Thomas M'Ewen, Bush Inn ; Mrs. Roach, Western Railway Hotel; J. Walduck, Queen's Arms Hotel; E. Landers Court House Hotel; G. Meiklejohn, Commercial Hotel; J. Walsh, Cornstalk Hotel; J. N. Bones, Tattersall's Hotel; C. Butler, Queensland Hotel; Thomas O'Sullivan, School of Arts Hotel; L. E. Johnson, Club Hotel.

Boarding Houses.—Mrs. Miles, Mrs. Schofield, Mrs. Pope. Tailors.—J. Sparks, McNaughton and Co., Bryant and McLean. Bootmakers.—S. R. N. Taudevin, O'Brien, A. C. Hoskins, J. Trappett, Watchmakers.—J. Sparks, W. Flavelle.

Carpenters, &c.—G. P. Williams, W. Edwards, A. B. Anderson, R. Clelland, F. A. Grigg. Saddlers.—Mat. Johnston, G. Wieneke, L. C. Johnson, C. Arnold, D. Crowley, J. Tredenick. Fruiterers.—J. C. Forrester, E. Pryor.

Tobacconists and Stationers.—J. Sparks, J. Warren, C. W. Conroy, H. J. Leitch.

Blacksmiths and Wheelwrights.—W. Miscamble, Ballard and Crawford, Federal Coach Works.

Gunsmith.—C. Martin Klaas.

Auctioneers.—T. A. Spencer, A. McPherson, E. H. Decker and Co., E. O'Connor, T. Walters.

Chemists.—J. Saunders, Davis' Western Drug and Dental Company.

Doctors.—G. S. L'Estrange, E. Sheaf. Dentists.—J. Saunders, C L. Davis, H. Care. Butchers.—H. Seitz, Cash Butchering Co.

Milliners.—Miss Davis, Miss Murray, Miss Worrall, Miss Meldon.

Tinsmiths, &c.—Lister and Hibberd, J. Warren.

Soap Manufacturer.—Mrs. F. Bourne.

Banks.—Bank of New South Wales—A. Bollman, Manager; Queensland National Bank—F. W. E.

Faithfull, Manager ; Bank of Australasia—J. S. Carlisle, Manager.
Solicitors.—R. H. Dyball, W. G. Mayne, F. W. S. Cumbrae Stewart.
Bakers.—H. J. Leitch, J. Hadwen, C. Crowley, L. J. Meldon.
Undertakers.—C. H. Hoffmann, J. Crawford.
Aerated Water Manufacturers.—Mrs. F. Bourne, H. O. Catling.
Newspaper.— Western Star, A. Robinson and Co. ; and Maranoa Advocate, H. Morgan.
Commission Agents.—T. A. Spencer, P. Browne, H. O. Catling, E. H. Decker and Co., E. O'Connor, Thos. Walters.
Painters.—J. England, H. M. Holloway,—Bootle.
Bicycle Depot.—C. W. Conroy."
(1902 Groom's Darling Downs book almanac, pp. 206-210)

1905 "Hodgson … to Lenroy mail service, and it was decided to recommend an open mail, and the Service to be extended about eight miles further up the creek than the present receiving office … Mr. Hewitt's motion, that a letter be written to the Railway Department requesting that the new siding at the Hodgson railway station be proceeded with." (Hodgson, 22 Feb 1905 , p.3)

Coach & mail conveyance

"Cobb's Coaches … A big gap exists between the time that the first of Cobb's coaches left Brisbane and the time that the last one returned. In that time a nation has almost been built, and the old line of coaches played a very big part in its building.

> Cobb's coaches could not wait for roads or bridges or crossings, they went out and made their own tracks for hundreds of miles. Rain, hail, or shine, mud dust or flood, it was all the same to Cobb's drivers and wild quiet, or medium quiet horses had to do their 'stage.'

The old thoroughbred coach was a wonderful contraption, and it was a red-letter day when it was brought into use. I ran into some old timers, the other day, men who had lived the better part of their lives along the tracks where Cobb's coaches used to travel, overlanders some of them, others were stockmen and horsebreakers." (Cobb's Coaches, 17 Jan 1925, p.17)

1866 – COBB AND CO. CONTRACT "Roma. December 13. Notwithstanding dull times, bad cheques, and torn calabashes, another store was opened last week to supply the wants of the Romans. Great satisfaction was expressed when it became known that Cobb and Co. had obtained the contract for carrying the mails between this and Brisbane. I am informed that their teams are now on the road with corn for the various depots about to be established along the line. There is some talk of their coaches running through from here to Dalby—180 miles in two days. If so, a clear saving of three days will be made in the delivery of the down mails, as now five days are consumed in that journey." (Roma, 22 Dec 1866, p.8)

COBB AND CO. INSPECTION AT ROMA "The mail from Brisbane arrived late last evening, two days behind time, but lately we have been so used to irregularity, that a matter of a day or so is not thought much of. Mr. Barns, of Cobb and Co., has just arrived on a visit of inspection, and hopes are entertained that we shall soon have that firm's coaches running right through. At the present time if one is not fortunate to be possessed of a quadruped that will carry him, he must make up his mind to walk between this and Dalby." (Roma, 8 Dec 1866, p.7) While earlier in 1866 "Nov. 17.— Telegraph line to Roma opened." (Queensland's Half Century 1859 to 1909 Notable Events, 8 Dec 1909, pp.23-37)

WESTERN MAIL RUN ALTERATION "Cobb and Co. In the early seventies the run from Dalby to Roma by coach took three days, and was divided into stages, the first being to Condamine township, the second stage from Condamine to Yuleba and the third from there to Roma. The fare … was £5 with an additional 2/6 for each meal and bed. Gangs of road agents infected the coaching routes in the '60's. One of the most notorious of the early bushrangers was McPherson, the 'Wild Scotsman,' who was finally apprehended after terrorising lonely settlers and travellers for a long period and sentenced … in 1866 to 25 years imprisonment." (Cobb and Co., 6 Jan 1949, p.4)

1867 – "COBB & CO.'S TELEGRAPHIC LINE OF ROYAL MAIL COACHES … Condamine and Roma, every Tuesday and Saturday at 8 a.m. Parcels booked through H. Barnes, Agent. Cobb & Co. Proprietors." (Advertising, 19 Mar 1867, p.4)

1867 – COACH BREAKDOWN "Rain here … has done a good deal of good … Mr. S. Bassett came to the Condamine with 7,000 sheep from Euthulla on the road to Tenterfield, but receiving a telegram from Roma, he has retraced his steps and gone back to Euthulla … Messrs. Cobb and Co.'s coach broke down about five miles this side of the Kogan, and the driver (Mr. McKenzie) had to go back there to get chains, &c., and managed to fasten the coach so as to proceed here. He reached here about ten o'clock; two hours late. The mail generally keeps capital time, and the letters are always given out at any time by Mr. King; certainly the most obliging postmaster I was ever brought into contact with in the colony." (Condamine, 5 Oct 1867, p.3)

1867 – ROMA TO CHARLEVILLE "Cobb and Co. have at length started their coach to and from Charleville and Roma, in pursuance of their mail contract … One benefit which we will derive … an easy means of transit … the measles are still holding their own in town … three little ones have succumbed … Very heavy rain fell on Monday at Eurella, Mount Abundance, and other stations, and also on Cattle Creek, much to the delight of the farmers … who have been at their wits end lately to find feed for their cattle… The Western road … has presented as bare an appearance as the much talked of road between Roma and Dalby." (Roma, 15 Jan 1876, p.2)

1869 – COACH WITH NO DRIVER "Roma. The arrival of Cobb and Co.'s coach with Her Majesty's mail is an event looked for twice a week with great interest by the inhabitants of Roma.

On Friday evening last, August 27th, while watching as usual for its appearance, they were startled by seeing

> the coach with a pair of horses galloping into town as hard as they could go, the reins broken, and not a soul in the vehicle.

Crashing along they went through the town—past the post office, past the booking office, avoiding the corners in the most miraculous way, until at last the horses were fairly encircled by horsemen, and finally stopped near the residence of the Police Magistrate. It appears that just as they came into town they shied at the Corporation unicycle (wheelbarrow), and the driver took a pull at them, when the rein broke in his band and the horses bolted. The driver immediately jumped out to get at them, but fell, and narrowly escaped having the coach over him, whilst a passenger managed to drop out behind with no other injury than a fright and severe shaking. It was a most fortunate thing that there were no more passengers ; had the trap been full a serious accident in all probability would have occurred. A lot of children were playing in the street, round the first corner, near where the horses bolted, and it is surprising that they escaped, as the horses dashed within a couple of feet of them in turning the corner." (Roma, 4 Sep 1869, p.4)

1873 – NEWLY PAINTED COACH "Condamine. Mr. Welch, Inspector of Telegraphs, passed through this on Friday, on his return from Cunnamulla, St. George, Roma, &c. Cobb and Co. have got a new coach radiant with fresh red paint and gold letters running on this line. If the coaches and horses are up to the mark, there will be no fear that the driver—Johnny Cunningham—will be up to time. He is a first-rate whip and a general favourite." (Condamine, 19 Apr 1873, p.4)

1875 – COACH ACCIDENT "An accident happened to Cobb and Co's coach on Sunday last which fortunately was unattended with any serious consequences. When passing Wallumbilla station the axle broke, rendering further progress impossible. Through the courtesy of Mr. Turbayne, the manager of the station, the driver was enabled to bring on the mail in a buggy ... I wish ... do something towards repairing the streets and putting the pavement ... If something is not done ... be a case of 'paddle your own canoe' (M'Dowall street) ... The weather lately has been splendid ... Amby Downs ... has commenced shearing operations ... Our stores are still short of necessaries." (Roma, 18 Sep 1875, p.3)

CRAMMED INTO COBB AND CO. COACH "Passenger Conveyance From Dalby To Roma. To the Editor of the Queensland Times. Sir,—For some time back the public have borne patiently with the style of conveyance provided by Cobb and Co. between the above named localities. In the coaches—a perfect nickname—three passengers are stowed away where there is room only for two, and so crammed is the space allotted for the feet with occasional bags of corn, as well as packages for which a high carriage in paid, that, setting aside danger, the journey has become a terror to travellers. From the Condamine horses and coach become worse, and, unfortunately ... a new driver has been put on in place of Mr. Cork, who resigned ... Yesterday a lady and her little baby had a most narrow escape. It appears the driver was 'indisposed,' and while the lady's husband and another gentleman were walking the driver brought the so-called coach foul of a stump or tree,

> pitching her clean out,

and sending the little innocent out of the mother's arms right amongst the horse's legs. Luckily the gentlemen were on foot, and they immediately rescued it from its dangerous position, when, to the surprise and delight of both parents, the little thing was found to be uninjured ... The whole line seems to be managed without regard to people's comfort or safety ... It was only this morning a gentleman told me of his being pitched three times from the coach during one journey. As there are to be some changes, I hope this letter will catch the manager's attention ... Seeing that we have a country 700 miles at the back of us, all of which has been eagerly taken up and, further, that large portions of it are superior to the Darling Downs—I think the Postmaster General might pay us a visit ... I will guarantee that we will give him a feed of beef and mutton such as cannot be produced on the Downs." (Original Correspondence, 2 Jan 1875, p.5)

1875 – TRAVELLED TO ROMA "Women's World ... In 1875 Mrs. E. E. Warner, who will celebrate her 81st birthday tomorrow, was a girl of only 19 when she left a large family of brothers and sisters to begin her married life with her husband, Canon Warner, in Queensland ... she has vivid memories of Queensland in its early days ... After their marriage in 1875 Canon and Mrs. Warner travelled by river to Ipswich, and then by the new railway to Dalby. From there, said Mrs. Warner, they went to Roma by one of Cobb and Co.'s coaches, travelling through the night. There were six horses to the coach, and at times there was no track to follow, and they just dodged between the tree trunks. Roma in those days was just a bush township, with a few rough wooden buildings that could hardly be called houses. The walls were unlined, and gave little protection from the fierce summer heat." (Women's World, 7 Apr 1936, p.25)

1877 – HALF-WAY HOUSE DULACCA "ROMA. (From the Western Star). We understand that the Minister for Works has expressed his intention of delaying the opening of the Western Railway Extension to Charley's Creek until the 1st of January next, thus giving Cobb and Co time to shift their stables, and complete the other arrangements necessary to carry on the service in their usual efficient style on the new route ... The coach journey will be accomplished in two days, the half-way house being at Dulacca; this will necessitate a complete alteration in the arrival and departure of the mails, and we would impress upon the postal authorities the importance of studying the convenience of the public of the district more than has been generally done in such alterations ... The Western mail, with the weekly papers, leaves Brisbane on Saturday morning, and ought to arrive here on Monday afternoon, thus rendering unnecessary what has always been considered an evil, the arrival and delivery of the Brisbane mail on Sundays.

The Charleville coach will doubtless leave on Tuesday, and thus the whole of the Western districts will get their mails a day earlier than at present ..."

DRIVING WITH HIS FEET "A gentleman recently arrived from Victoria has expressed to us his admiration of the quality and condition of the horses on this line ; he noticed, however, one novelty that he does not consider an improvement—

a Cobb's coachman who uses his feet in driving as much as his hands !

He prefers the old style, as he does not believe in the reins being manipulated by the feet." (Roma, 8 Dec 1877, p.3)

1882 – QUEENSLAND CONVEYANCE OF MAILS "Tenders for the services, 1883-4-5 ... 134. Roma and Surat, via Rocky Bank, Deepwater, Trinidad, Yalebone Saw-mills, and Oberina, by horse, once a week, for one, two, or three years." (The Queenslander, 29 Jul 1882, p.155)

1902 – THE STOPPAGE OF COBB AND CO. "The stoppage of the Queensland mails by the breakdown of Cobb and Co., makes a crisis in the settlement of the western districts of Queensland, as well as in the drought. The succession of dry seasons has thrown this firm into difficulties with the fulfilment of their network of contracts ... Cobb and Co., abandoned their contracts, and the interior was left without means of transit ... In the gold days in the Eastern States, the coaches went to the accompaniment of armed troopers. Now without that picturesque accessory, the coaches face all the dangers of flood and fire, and form part of the thin tie that binds many an outback settlement to the railway terminus. The country cannot do without them, and the even temporary suspension that has taken place, is a proof that someone has blundered ... Australia has learned many things, but not how to handle a drought ... Australian stock ... fades away when the rains do not come. The loss by the drought is estimated at 40,000,000 sheep and cattle, and there is no saying what it may reach if the weather does not break soon." (The Stoppage of Cobb and Co., 17 May 1902, p.48)

Mail 'Bail Up!'

1865 – ROBBERY OF THE ROMA MAIL. "On Tuesday morning the Roma mail was 'stuck up' in a brigalow scrub, between Blythedale and Roma, and robbed of everything worth taking." (Robbery of the Roma Mail, 4 Nov 1865, p.3)

BAIL UP "A Maranoa Reminisence. The 'Wild Scotchman.' Opening of the Queensland Bank, Roma ... thirty years ago. In 1865 Mr. Mallon was engaged hawking. He says : —I was travelling with my drays and two men up the Dawson, between Taroom (then known as Bonner's Knob) and Roma, when I heard ... that the Roma mailman had been stuck up and robbed of £1,600 ... it was the 'Wild Scotchman' ... About two days after that ... I saw my two men with their hands up alongside the dray and a tall man a few paces off covering them with a gun. He had seen me first and shouted to me to come on and 'bail up' too ...

'O it's the Scotchman' I said ... *'All the money I have is in the cash box in the tail of the tray and you're welcome to it'* ... He only wanted a feed, and a change of clothes for which he said he would pay ... I learned afterwards that these ... half-crowns were part of the consignment of money that had been sent up to open the first Queensland Bank in Roma." (A Maranoa Reminiscence, 27 Mar 1895, p.3)

1867 – BAIL UP OF MAILMAN "We appear to be bailed up here. Cobb and Co.'s mailman made his appearance this morning, but he only brought one Condamine mail ; none from Dalby or Brisbane. He reports the country as impassable, judging, no doubt, from the non-appearance of the Dalby mailman at Condamine. We are now without our down country letters for a fortnight. And they say that the railway is under water for miles. Is this railway ever to benefit us! Permanently, I mean. I very much doubt it. Cheap railways never paid as yet ...

The Bungil and Bungeworgerai creeks are not high, so we could not have had so much rain up here, as they have been favored with down country. No mail, no news, so expect but little from me. The Romans hearing of a pretty little 'job,' in Government clearing Bowen street where there is very little or no traffic, and not clearing M'Donald street, wherein all the buildings connected with business are situated ... Be it remarked that Bowen-street would cost in clearing considerably less than McDowell-street, and is not the direct road from the bridge over the Bungil to the bridge over the Bungewargerai ... the racecourse will be fenced in before long ... The hospital was also touched upon ... letter ... on behalf of the inhabitants of the town and district of Roma the urgent necessity for a (sic.) hospital in that town." (Roma, 23 May 1867, p.3)

1870 – MAIL DELAYED "Roma ... Her Majesty's mails, per Cobb and Company, arrived this evening, and the Romans, having received no Brisbane news since Friday, the 8th instant, were pleased enough to hear the well-known sound of the post-horn. An untoward accident, which occurred about fifteen miles from the Condamine, occasioned an additional day's delay ... the buildings in connection with the national school are steadily progressing." (Roma, 26 Mar 1870, p.3)

THE ROBBERY OF SILVER FROM ONE OF COBB'S COACHES. "The Queensland Express relates that a few weeks ago the Bank of New South Wales sustained a loss of £100 through a bag of silver having been carelessly left in one of Cobb and Co.'s coaches by the driver (Martin), to whom the money had been entrusted for conveyance to the branch bank at Roma.

The bag disappeared most mysteriously ...

About a week ago Sergeant Francis, of the Ipswich constabulary, received some information which led him to suspect that the cash had found its way into the hands of a man named McDermott, a groom employed at Tattersall's Hotel, Ipswich ... it was found ... but nothing like the amount lost by the bank." (The Robbery of Silver from One of Cobb's Coaches, 9 Feb 1870, p.4)

ca. 1866 Women and children at Bindango Station, near Roma – Courtesy State Library of Queensland

1860 Bush hut Roma, sawn timber slabs covering roof and verandah – Courtesy State Library of Queensland

ca. 1870-1880 Station hands on a property near Roma – Courtesy State Library of Queensland

a. 1877 McDowall Street, Roma – Courtesy State Library of Queensland

ca. 1880-1890 Avenue of trees along McDowall Street, Roma (in Western Qld)
– Courtesy State Library of Queensland

1882 Roma passenger station – Courtesy State Library of Queensland

ca. 1915 Quiet street scene in McDowall Street, Roma 'There is room for you and opportunity for you in Queensland' – Courtesy State Library of Queensland

1875 Post and Telegraph Office, Roma – Courtesy State Library of Queensland

Roma's oil and gas

The story of Roma's oil and gas development is one of early promise, technical challenges, and dramatic events.

BAD LUCK "Bad luck seems to dog the search for oil in Queensland. Some years ago the first Roma oil well was blocked by tools falling into the drill-hole ; and a second caught fire. Now we have news of the death of the superintendent of the Longreach well. After two attempts to blow in the oil had failed owing to the explosive not acting, the superintendent proceeded to make an extra large 'torpedo' of gelignite, taking the precaution of ordering all workmen out of reach while he fixed the detonator. The 'torpedo' exploded prematurely and blew the superintendent to bits. — 'Muttaburra'." (No Title, 28 Oct 1931, p6)

While in 1907, the town's early experience with natural gas was recalled. "ROMA GAS BORE … It will be remembered that when a bore was sunk for water gas showed itself and after running to waste for a couple of years it was run into a gasometer and the town reticulated for the purpose of a gas supply. In a few days, however, the gas supply failed, and the efforts made to restore the supply were aborted. A company was formed to sink for oil in the vicinity and its bore is down 400ft." (Roma Gas Bore, 3 Sep 1907, p.11)

The year before, in 1906, efforts were already underway to bring gas to buildings. "ROMA GAS WORKS … Mr. Henderson, hydraulic engineer, arrived in Roma on Saturday evening last on a visit, of inspection in connection with the gas works. During Monday he was employed inspecting the work already carried out, particularly in connection with the gasometer, and giving instructions for carrying out, one or two necessary alterations. It is expected that the work will be finished about the end of next week, and he will then again visit Roma for the purpose of seeing if everything has been completed satisfactorily, and if so, to hand the works over to the council, which will then have to proceed with the work of getting the gas to the buildings … The matter of the erection of a house for the gas governor and of the fence round the works was left in the hands of Mr. Henderson and the Mayor." (Roma Gas Works, 10 May 1906, p.2)

Soon after, the price for gas was set. "ROMA GAS PLANT. Our Roma correspondent writes :—At a special meeting of the Municipal Council the price for gas was fixed for lighting purposes at 6s. per 1000ft., and for cooking at 5s. per 1000ft. Mr. J. B. Henderson will visit Roma on Tuesday to hand over the gas plant to the council." (Roma Gas Plant, 28 May 1906, p.4)

However, technical issues soon emerged. "ROMA GAS … At a special meeting of the Town Council to-day it was decided to wire the Premier requesting that an expert be sent with a view to ascertaining whether the failure of gas was due to natural causes or to an obstruction at the bottom of the bore." (Roma Gas, 19 Jun 1906, p.40)

Unexpectedly, the gas bore began to show signs of oil. "STRUCK OIL AT ROMA. Residents at Roma received a rude shock on Saturday night, when it became known that the supply of gas had decreased. The familiar noise in the bore was absent, and investigation proved that the gasometer had lowered three feet, and water from the separator in the by-pass was covered with oil.

The Mayor and aldermen inspected the plant on Sunday, and ordered the pipe connecting the bore with the separator to be removed. It was found that the bore no longer vomited gas and water, but water mixed with oil. The opinion is that by confinement the gas forced another subterranean passage and released the oil, but not in sufficient quantities to be of commercial value. The Secretary of the Oil Company is beseiged by persons desirous of taking shares in the Company." (Struck Oil at Roma, 23 Jun 1906, p.8)

This discovery was followed by further signs of an oil spring. "OIL AT ROMA. The stoppage of the gas supply from the bore has been followed by a slight discharge of what appears to be kerosene. Though the discharge is not of any commercial value, it is sufficient to prove that somewhere in the earth below there is an oil spring which, if tamed, might prove of more value than the gas that has been lost. As the result of the appearance of oil at the bore shares in the company that was formed some time ago to bore for oil in the vicinity are eagerly sought for, and a further issue of 4000 additional shares has been found necessary to meet the demand." (Oil at Roma, 23 Jun 1906, p.11)

Despite the excitement, the town had to return from gas lighting back to the hurricane lamp. "ROMA GAS BORE. Still no report has been received by the Roma Town Council from the officials who were entrusted with the experiments at the Roma gas bore a fortnight ago (says yesterday's Roma 'Star'). The council are waiting to see if the officials have any recommendations to make, and whether the Treasurer approves of same, before they prepare to take action themselves. In the meantime, the week's supply of gas which remains in the gasometer has been conserved for use during next week, to give visitors to town in connection with the annual show and races an opportunity of seeing what a splendid natural light has been won and lost—it is hoped only temporarily lost—at Roma. It is almost pathetic at present to see the large light in M'Dowall-street. 600 candle power in strength, replaced by a hurricane lamp of perhaps two-match power." (Roma Gas Bore, 12 Jul 1906, p.4)

By 1907, the financial strain on the council was growing. "ROMA GAS BORE. Owing to the delay in restoring the supply of gas in the bore sunk at Roma, the local council has been feeling the weight of the loan required to reticulate the town. An application was made to the Government to have the interest charge abolished in the meantime, but the Treasurer has declined to accede to the request, and has decided that the council must abide by the bargain made." (Roma Gas Bore, 1 Jul 1907, p.7)

In 1908, drilling continued with some optimism. ROMA GAS BORE. "Satisfactory progress continues to be made at the sinking of the bore for mineral oil. On Friday the depth reached was 3,123 feet, being 5 feet since noon on Tuesday. On Thursday night a stratum of that hard grey shale was met with, but now the considerable thickness of some 2,000 feet of it has been gone through it is hoped the belt being drilled on Friday is, like some of the others, only a thin bar occurring in the sandy and softer formation.

All being well, in the course of a month or so, some of the gas met with in the previous bore should be reached." (Roma Gas Bore, 29 Jun 1908, p.5)

That same year, a dramatic event occurred. "MINERAL OIL AT ROMA EXPLOSION OF GAS ... Tuesday Telegrams were received in Brisbane reporting that the Mineral Oil Company's bore at Roma struck gas at a depth of 3680 feet. The pressure of gas was very powerful, and as a strong wind was blowing the gas ignited. The flames rose to a height estimated at from 60 to 100 feet. The gas was ignited by a boiler and the attendants were unable to extinguish it. The shareholders in the Company are elated at the gas having been struck, but doubt is expressed by some as to whether it can be extinguished. LATER. The latest news from Roma concerning the fire in the Oil Company's bore, state that the derrick was buckled up and all the plant was destroyed. The gas continued to issue in increasing volume, and the roar of the flames can he heard for a distance of seven miles. The heat is so intense that it is impossible to approach within 60 feet of the bore. The Minister for Mines with the Hydraulic Engineer and manager of the International Well Boring Company held a consultation to-night with the result that the Boring Company will immediately commence to work a contrivance which is hoped will smother the flames. It is the intention of the Company to smother the flames and continue the boring, as it is expected that a good flow of oil will be struck 300 feet lower down. A telegram was received by the Minister for Mines to-night from the Secretary of the Company stating that the Engineer and contractor both reported that oil was now flowing from the bore, but the flames were increasing in volume." (Mineral Oil at Roma Explosion of Gas, 28 Oct 1908, p.2)

The cause of the explosion was later determined. "THE ROMA GAS EXPLOSION. The man to discover that gas was escaping in large quantities was riding past at the time, and stopped his horse while filling up his pipe from a tin of Referee flake cut tobacco, and noticed the smell and galloped on until he came to the Referee tobacco sign post at the cross roads, when the explosion look place." (The Roma Gas Explosion, 30 Nov 1908, p.7)

The event was described as "HOLOCAUST ON HOSPITAL HILL. On Hospital Hill, half a mile from the town of Roma, at 9.15 a.m. on October 27, 1908, the quietude of the rural surroundings were shattered without warning by an amazing, vibrating, booming roar such as no Australian had ever heard before ... Australia's first petroliferous gas well fire (QG No. 3, also known as R.O.M. No.1) had crashed into being ... Heat was so intense that grass in a paddock 100 yards was scorched almost black. Within a few minutes all machinery near to the hole was reduced to ruins ... The flame subsided, and at 10p.m. on December 11 gave a final flicker and was out. Thus ended Roma's world-famous well fire that had burned for nearly seven weeks." (The Roma Story, 1965, p.3)

Drilling continued in 1910. "ROMA GAS BORES. At the gas bore to-day the men succeeded in gripping the 4in. casing of the 1700ft level, and lifted it 18m (our Roma correspondent wired last night) ... the water issuing from the casing is frothy and mixed with gas ... The Grafton Range bore has reached a depth of 700ft." (Roma Gas Bores, 23 Feb 1910, p.4)

In 1914, there was renewed optimism "OIL AT ROMA ... *a township on the western Darling Downs, in Queensland, is going to be the centre of a second Pennsylvania oil field.* So says Mr. B. J. Webber, who has had 26 years experience boring on oil and gas fields from east to west in the United States, and throughout Galicia, Romania, West Africa, and New Zealand. Mr. Webber has been investigating the Roma field, and he speaks in glowing terms of its oil and gas prospects, *The field is that good,* he states, *that I have already secured 500 (?) acres for boring rights for my syndicate ... I have bored the world's greatest fields, and I honestly think that Roma is going to a second Pennsylvania. The formations compare well, being made up of sandstone, shale, and streaks of coal overlying the gas, and oil ... It will certainly be an oilfield ... The plant which I am using at Roma is the greatest success known as a borer through all kinds of formations. It is being built in Sydney, and will shortly be in action ... If gas should be met with at Roma ... it could easily be piped to Brisbane or Sydney.*" (Oil at Roma, 17 Jun 1914, p.4)

By 1915, preparations for further boring were nearly complete. "OIL AT ROMA. The preparation of the plant for boring for oil at Roma is well forward, and it is hoped that boring operations will be commenced in a fortnight." (Oil at Roma, 3 Dec 1915, p.4)

In the following decade, public commentary reflected both expectation and caution. "ROMA GAS. Sir,—The striking of natural gas at Roma, at more than one place, was fully to be expected, but it is to be hoped that the importation of expensive plants for the extraction of petrol will not be continued, because it is unnecessary ... There is in Wickham-street, Brisbane, a company called the Kitson Light Company, who use a cylinder ... Don't see why small cylinder of compressed gas could not be used in illuminating lamps with incandescent mantles.—I am, sir, &c, W.C.W. Bribie Island, October 14." (Roma Gas, 18 Oct 1928, p.3)

In 1929, boring progress. "ROMA OIL ... The secretary of Queensland Roma Oil, Ltd. (Mr. E. W. Hammond), reports: *As expected, boring progress has been very rapid since the 500ft. level was reached. A report from the supervising borer, Mr. Jason Tichborne, shows that the bore is now down to a depth of 690ft. Soft black shale is still being encountered.*" (Roma Oil. Queensland Roma Oil, 10 Jan 1929, p.6)

The year 1950 saw GAS STILL FLOWING AT ROMA with yet another dramatic gas explosion."Gas and water are still pouring from the 760- feet bore, which exploded into flames, and injured four people yesterday, 35 miles east of Roma on Hillside station ... The fire, which reached a height of 70 feet above the borehead was put out to-day at 4.30 p.m., when a vacuum was created above the borehead by the battery explosion of a five pound tube of gelignite. Oil scientist, Mr. Derek Pitnan, a party of trained oil men, and local police rigged a flying fox over the bore and used it to move the gelignite into position." (Gas still at Roma, 11 May 1950, p. 3)

1904 ROMA BORE GAS "The treasurer stated yesterday that he had promised the Roma Town Council a loan of £7,000 odd to reticulate the town, in order to take advantage of the gas escaping from the bore; and without doubt, this would be granted." (Roma Bore Gas, 29 Apr 1904, p.4)

Above: 1919 The state oil bore at Roma, showing works in December last (C. W. D. Savage) – The Queenslander, Brisbane, 22 February 1919, p.25

Below: ca. 1927 Aerial view of Roma Oil Bore (Fairfax) – Courtesy National Library of Australia

Opposite page: ca. 1927 Oilfields at Roma – Courtesy State Library of Queensland

1950 ROMA BORE EXPLOSION "These exclusive photographs to the Brisbane Telegraph show the spectacular scene caused by a bore gas explosion at Hillside grazing property, 30 miles north-east of Roma on Tuesday afternoon. Explosive gas which erupted suddenly from the 760 feet deep bore, burst into flames which rose 100 feet into the air. Four people were burned by the explosion which followed the string of a match 60 feet away from the hole which had been gushing water for nearly 18 hours. Oil experts extinguished the flames nearly 14 hours later by exploding gelignite over the hole. Gas subsequently poured from the bore which was cordoned off. Oil experts will make definite tests to determine whether the explosion has any particular significance in the search for oil. Four victims of the explosion - S. P. C. Rusbrook, 43, owner of Hillside; Maxwell Goebel, 19, boring contractor, of Louisa Street, Toowoomba; Perry Goebel, 9, Max's brother and Allan Buchanan, 18, well borer are in Roma hospital in a satisfactory condition." (Brisbane Telegraph, 12 May 1950, p.14)

from the bore shoot 70 feet into the air shortly before a gelignite charge ed over the hole, the blast of which extinguished the flame. On the right water shoots sky high with flames from the bore.

A 44-gallon drum is thrown over the bore casing in an attempt to put out the flame but it only succeeded in spreading the fire, hastening destruction of the plant valued at more than £1,000.

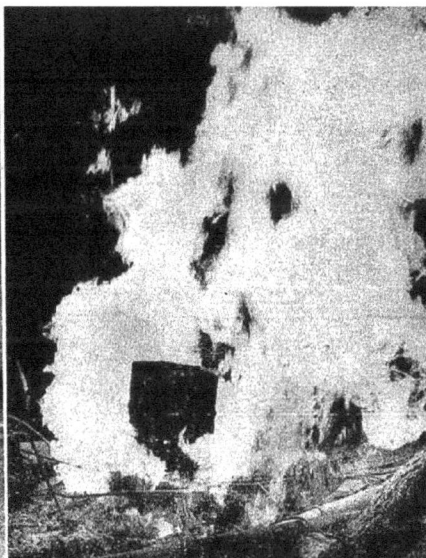

The fire spreads through the plant destroying the drilling gear and a truck which could not be moved because it was out of petrol.

is left of the truck and the boring plant after they had been swept by the intense

ROMA BORE EXPLOSION

THESE exclusive photographs to the Brisbane Telegraph show the spectacular scene caused by a bore gas explosion at Hillside grazing property, 30 miles north-east of Roma on Tuesday afternoon. Explosive gas which erupted suddenly from the 760 feet deep bore, burst into flames which rose 100 feet into the air.

Four people were burned by the explosion which followed the striking of a match 60 feet away from the hole which had been gushing water for nearly 18 hours. Oil experts extinguished the flames nearly 14 hours later by exploding gelignite over the hole.

Gas subsequently poured from the bore which was cordoned off. Oil experts will make definite tests to determine whether the explosion has any particular significance in the search for oil.

Four victims of the explosion—S. P. C. Rusbrook, 43, owner, of Hillside; Maxwell Goebel, 19, boring contractor, of Louisa Street, Toowoomba; Perry Goebel, 9, Max's brother, and Allan Buchanan, 18, well borer—

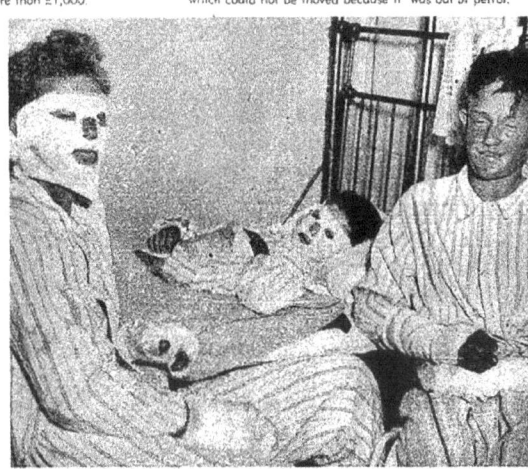

Three of the four victims of the explosion in the Roma hospital. In bed is Perry Goebel, aged nine, at the head of the bed is Allan Buchanan and on the left Maxwell Goebel, whose clothing caught alight after he struck a match 60 feet from the bore hole.

ca. 1910 Oil Bore in Roma – Courtesy Flickr

ca. 1906 Roma Gas Works, apparatus for separating natural gas from artesian water – Courtesy State Library of Queensland

ca. 1935 View of floodwaters of Myall Creek as seen from the Roma Oil derrick, Dalby – Courtesy State Library of Queensland

ca. 1928 Chrysler sedan running on Roma oil, Roma – Courtesy State Library of Queensland

The Big Rig: Oil and Gas Museum and 'Lenroy' Slab Hut

Today in Roma, visitors can explore *The Big Rig*, a museum dedicated to Australia's living history of oil and gas exploration. As part of the site, you'll find the historic 'Lenroy' slab hut, originally located on Clark's Creek at 'Lenroy', Hodgson, Queensland. This hut, which dates back to the late 1800s, served as a home to many families over the decades. For more information on its original location. See *Appendix 2.8: Old Slab Hut Original Site—Parish of Hodgson, County of Waldegrave, Map*

Keegan Family

ORIGINAL SELECTOR THOMAS KEEGAN "Obituary ... Mr. Jonathan Keegan ... With his father, the late Mr. Thomas Keegan, they were the first men to acquire land in the Dargal district, his father selecting Dolleriene (now Lenroy)." (Obituary Mr. Jonathan Keegan, 3 May 1946, p.5)

1912 "Mr. John Thomas Keegan passed away at Roma on Tuesday evening, at the age of 66 years ... came to Queensland in, 1880. He first went to St. George and afterwards to Mitchell ... Subsequently he went to Hodgson, and was the first selector on Dargal Creek ... He had been a resident of Dargal Creek for 16 years ... He leaves a widow and a family, of five daughters and four sons, the daughters being Mrs. Steve Walsh, Mrs. Fred. Johnson, Mrs. Duncan Lines, all of whom reside in this district, and Mrs. Hopgood and Mrs. Baldwin, of Tenterfield, N.S.W. The sons are Messrs. Josh Keegan, of Roma, and Messrs. Jonathan, Edward, and Patrick Keegan, who are selectors on Dargal Creek." (Land Office Appointment, 2 Nov 1912, p.2)

1936 "Old Roma Resident's Death ... Mrs. Harriet Keegan ... in 1867 she married the late Mr. J. T. Keegan, and came to Queensland in 1880 ... in 1884 her husband selected land at Muckadilla, and later was one of the first settlers on the Dargal, near Hodgson." (Old Roma Resident's Death, 23 Jul 1936, p.19)

Resident families 'Lenroy'

(Information from Electoral Roll, unless otherwise stated)

- 1893, Keegan (Source unknown) Dolleriene/Dollerene
- 1903 BYRNE Keyran, Matthew, May Margaret Isabella, Glenroy, Clark's Creek
- 1905 BYRNE Matthew, May Margaret Isabella, Glenroy, Clark's Creek
- 1906 BYRNE Matthew, May Margaret Isabella, Glenroy, Clark's Creek
- 1906 BYRNE Margaret—Bi-monthly Electoral List (Advertising, 9 Jun 1906, p.5), Lenroy, Clark's Creek
- 1907 BYRNE
- 1908 FALLON John Joseph, Jennie Louise, Lenroy, Hodgson
- 1909 FALLON John Joseph, Jennie Louise, Lenroy, Hodgson
- 1912 RYAN Michael John, Miriam Agnes, Lenroy, Hodgson
- 1913 RYAN Michael John, Miriam Agnes Lenroy, Hodgson
- 1914 R. E. HUNT (Sale of Qld Sheep Property, 2 Feb 1914)
- 1914 LYNNE
- 1915 LYNNE John, Ella Brenda Lenroy, Hodgson
- 1916 LYNNE John, Ella Brenda Lenroy, Hodgson
- 1917 LYNNE John, Ella Brenda Lenroy, Hodgson
- 1919 LYNNE John, Ella Brenda Lenroy, Hodgson
- 1920 PROPSTING Hadley Melville & Mabel (Advertising, 18 Aug 1920, p.4)
- 1920 NEILD—leasee
- 1922 JOHNSON bought from Lynne (see below), Lenroy Dargal Creek
- 1925 & 1926 JOHNSON Gladys Isabel, Lenroy, Hodgson
- 1928 JOHNSON Norman Ernest, Lenroy, Hodgson
- 1930 & 1932 JOHNSON Norman Ernest, Lenroy, Hodgson
- 1937 JOHNSON Cecil Wyman (Advertising, 15 Aug 1936, p.3)
- 1934 & 1936 JOHNSON Henry John, Lenroy, Hodgson
- 1943 JOHNSON Percy Douglas Lenroy,
- Hodgson
- 1949 JOHNSON Percy Douglas, Kenneth Victor, Lenroy, Hodgson
- 1954 JOHNSON Percy Douglas, Kenneth Victor, Mavis Rosa, Lenroy, Hodgson
- 1958 JOHNSON Percy Douglas, Kenneth Victor, Mavis Rosa, Lenroy, Hodgson

1907 – BYRNE—Fowl Story "On The Land. I noticed in the 'Western Star' some time ago (writes Mrs. Margaret Byrne, of Lenroy, Hodgson) that a white Leghorn hen had laid an uncommonly large egg. It appears wonders of this kind will never cease. I have a Leghorn hen that laid two fully developed eggs within a minute of each other. From this it seems the Leghorn fowl is wonderfully prolific." (On the Land, 27 Feb 1907, p.2) Another mention in 1914 "Dargal Creek. (From Our Correspondent.) Cattle dealers are operating freely in this district at the present time. Mr. Kyran Byrne, at one time a Dargal resident but now of Mungallala, has within the last few weeks purchased about 300 head of cattle from Hodgson and Dargal farmers." (Dargal Creek, 25 Apr 1914, p.3)

1909 – FALLON "Pastoral Matters. Charlleville, January 12. McPhie and Co., Charleville, report the sale, on account of Mr. G. E. Bunning, of 1300 wethers; also, on account of J. Fallon, Lenroy, Hodgson, 1700 wethers" (Pastoral Matters, 13 Jan 1909, p.6)

1914 – LYNE "From John Lyne, Lenroy, Hodgson, applying for the lease in front of his house to enable him to make a garden and tennis court as his house was on a stony, ridge with the creek behind, and there was no room.—Permission granted." (Bungil Shire Council, 3 Oct 1914, p.2) and in 1915 "Dargal Creek. The continued dry weather is now causing much concern ...

I understand that Mr. Oarles, of the Upper Dargal, and Mr. Lyne of Lenroy, have arranged with Mr. Chapman, the sub-artesian well contractor, to sink a bore for each of them" (Dargal Creek, 14 Jul 1915, p.3)

1920 – PROPSTING "Propsting, Hadley Melville, Lenroy, Hodgson, grazier ... Propsting, Mabel, Lenroy, Hodgson, domestic duties." (Advertising, 18 Aug 1920, p.4) "Fatal Accident.—A very sad ceremony was witnessed at Bindango on Monday morning last, when the body of Guy Nield, of Lenroy, Hodgson, was laid in the Bindango private cemetery. The deceased was, only a recent settler in the district, having about two years ago purchased from Mr. Propsting the lease and stock on Lenroy." (Advertising, 7 Jul 1920, p.2)

JOHNSON FAMILY

1922 – LENROY SALE "Sale of Grazing Property.— H. M. Campbell and Co. have just effected the sale of Lenroy, a nice grazing selection near Hodgson, comprising about 4000 acres, on account of Mr. J. Lyne, at a very satisfactory figure, Mr. H. J. Johnson being the purchaser." Henry's wife, Ann Benyon Rayner, was the daughter of Mr. and Mrs. Benjamin Raynor. Raynor owned the Royal Hotel at Hodgson. (Germans Depressed, 22 Apr 1922, p.2)

1922 – "ROMA METHODIST CIRCUIT ... Minister: Rev. A. C. Tempest Roma (Bungil-st.) ... Ferndale ... Mitchell ... Wallumbilla and Pickanjinnie ... Glenroy, Dargal : Monday, July 3rd, 8 p.m.; Amby: Friday, July 7th, 8 p.m. Rev. A. C. Tempest." (Advertising, 1 Jul 1922, p.3)

1927 "PRESENTATION.—A very pleasant function took place on the afternoon of Wednesday last, the 6th instant, at, 'Lenroy,' the hospitable home of Mr. and Mrs. H. J. Johnson on Dargal Creek. The occasion was a presentation from their Dargal friends to the Rev F. and Mrs. Chowns, of the Roma Methodist Circuit, on the eve of their departure to their future sphere of labour at East Brisbane." (The Western Star, 14 Apr 1927, p.2)

1927 – WEDDING "Hodgson. From our correspondent. May 9. Wedding.—A popular and attractive wedding was celebrated on Thursday, the 5th instant, at the Roma Methodist Church. The contracting parties were Mr. William Harold Cary ... and Miss Gladys Isabel Johnson, second daughter of Mr. and Mrs. H. J. Johnson, of 'Lenroy,' Dargal Creek ... The bride looked very graceful in a white marietta frock handsomely beaded and showing effects of shirring and French pleating. She wore a beautiful veil, lent by her sister-in-law, Mrs. V. Johnson ... After the marriage ceremony the bridal party returned by cars to 'Lenroy,' 20 miles distant, where the dainty breakfast was served on the long verandah ... The bridegroom's gift to the bride was a marble clock, and to each bridesmaid a gold brooch. The bride's present to the bridegroom is to be selected on the honeymoon." (Hodgson, 14 May 1927, p.2)

1936 – OBITUARY. MR. H. J. JOHNSON. (13/2/1869-1/8/1936) "By the death of Mr. H. J. Johnson, 'Lenroy,' Hodgson, the Roma district has lost one of its finest type of selectors, and a man who had spent the best years of his life in industrious and enterprising work in the district, and the State generally has become richer for that industry. Born at Hockley, Warwickshire, England, in 1869, the late Mr. Johnson, as a youth of 18 years, sailed with his parents, brothers and sisters, on the sailing ship 'Eastminster' early in October, 1887, and after sixteen weeks voyage landed at Maryborough on 2nd January, 1888 ... From Maryborough, the Johnson family came to Roma, where Mr. Johnson secured his first employment at Bourne's Cordial Factory, along with Mr. Frank Mullavey, of Roma. But big ambition was for the land, and he secured his next job with the late Mr. James Nimmo, at Hodgson, and while there he selected his first venture in land, 48 acres in Hodgson in 1891. In 1893 he married Miss Ann Benyon Rayner, and started on his wheat-growing career by planting 20 acres, three years later. He followed up shearing during the wheat-growing season, and later, in partnership with James Stevenson, and then Reuben Plummer, carried on contract tank-sinking in all corners of the Maranoa district. In 1911, after securing further wheat lands at Hodgson and grazing land on the Donnybrook, he turned his attention to combining sheep with wheat growing. In 1920 Mr. Johnson produced 3800 bags of wheat, besides over 100 tons of hay, and at the time, was the largest individual wheat producer in the Maranoa, if not Queensland. Mr. Johnson was always an advocate for water and fodder conservation, which practice is in evidence by the water facilities on each of his properties, and the two large haysheds which stand at Hodgson filled with hay. In 1922 Lenroy was purchased, and which under his management now ranks among the best improved properties in the district. He always took a keen interest in the breeding of good stock. Although during his later years he could not do any active work, he was always looked to for his sound advice ... He leaves a widow, four sons and four daughters to mourn their loss. The sons are Messrs. Cecil, Victor, Norman and Douglas, and the daughters are Mrs. Wm. Stinson, 'Moscow,' Roma, Mrs. W. H. Cary, Hendra, Brisbane, and Mrs. V. Andrews, and Mrs. D. Dickie, of Hodgson." (Obituary. Mr. H. J. Johnson, 8 Aug 1936, p.2)

1946 – "JOHNSON—CARTER. The Engagement is announced of Mavis Rosa, younger Daughter of Mr. & Mrs. A. J. Carter, Hendra to Kenneth Victor, only Son of Mr. & Mrs. Vic. Johnson, Lenroy, Hodgson, via Roma." (Family Notices, 28 Dec 1946, p.4)

1950s – "KENNETH VICTOR JOHNSON AND MAVIS ROSA CARTER were married 29 November 1947 and were the last occupants of the old slab hut. Ken and Mavis' son, Kevin Johnson, recalls the hut, or their home, was made from unsealed hand cut cypress pine with wire and hessian on the ceiling. The house was built on stumps and the floor was timber. The door latches were made from string threaded through holes in the doors to lift the metal latch on the inside. Originally, there was no glass in the windows or corrugated iron on the roof, these being added sometime after the original hut was built. There were three rooms, and a verandah wrapped around three sides.

There were no doors onto the eastern verandah. A kitchen was added to the south-western veranda (with a crown stove), as was a bathroom on the northern side. Ken later would say *the bathroom was the coldest in Australia.* There are no recollections by the family as to whether the bathroom had hot water. There was a large dining room where meals were served to the shearers, the original shearing shed was located across Clark's Creek, being visible from the house. Later another building was added which housed the 32 volt generator. Doug Johnson told the story of how they used a tipping dray to move bottle trees to the house site. Ellen (Ken's mother) would measure the girth of the bottle trees every Christmas. Although the house was close to the creek, it was never known to have flooded. Two wells existed to supply water for the home—one on the creek and the other near the original cattle yards. The house boasted a tennis court and large vegetable garden (1914) and a garage was also built at the site (date unknown). Beside the old slab hut a new residence was added (date unknown). Before Ken was married, Ken and his parents Victor Henry and Ellen Rita Johnson lived in the newer addition. The extended residence features in the background of Victor and Ellen's wedding photo. After Ken's parents left the property, Ken relocated the newer addition more centrally on the property, on to an area containing stands of cypress pine and sandy loam soil. From 1952 onwards, the old slab hut was left vacant and deteriorated over time. Ken and Mavis decided to preserve the heritage building. They sold the old slab hut to local artist John Morrison 'for a song' (or rather a painting). The old slab hut left 'Lenroy' for its new home at Roma Villa, in 1980, for use as a venue for art and craft sales. Later, the old slab hut was again relocated, this time to the site of The Big Rig, Roma.

1888 – BENJAMIN RAYNER, Father of Ann Benyon Johnson "Silver Wedding at Hodgson. A social event, exciting great interest in the West, was celebrated at Hodgson, near Roma, on the 14th inst. It was the silver wedding of Mr. and Mrs. B. Rayner, who are very popular and highly-respected throughout Maranoa and well-known in Ipswich and Brisbane. As the evening of St. Valentine's Day closed in numerous buggies, driven by handsome rein-beaux and bearing many lovely fares, might be observed entering the township inn-ward bound. Of the invited guests, a distinguished company ... including the Mayor of Roma and other notabilities ... assembled in the Royal Hotel, and ... dined together. The large hall was decorated with greenery, and a number of colored mottoes, such as 'Welcome to all,' 'Hearty good wishes,' 'Laugh and grow fat,' and so on, were displayed on the walls. Toothsome life-preservers, in the shape of choice viands, rich liquors and delicious fruit were supplied profusely and in a-bun-dance. Some of the grapes were as large as plums. The reigners of Hodgson are noted for their generosity, and their company on this occasion were Regaled in a truly royal hospitable style. Several very merry chaff-makers enlivened the meal with their jokelets. The capacity of some for supplying tongue wittily and gracefully was duly appreciated. The sumptuous and costly feast having received due attention, and the glasses being charged with frothing champagne, the genial Mr. J. H. Irwin rose ... proposing the health of Mr. and Mrs. Rayner on this auspicious occasion. He had known them over fifteen years, and always found them honorable and estimable ... Many more would have been with them had not the wet weather of the previous few days prevented ... Then followed the dissection of the bride-cake, a little mountain snowy white, and crowned with a garland of white flowers ... the sweet mountain was speedily distributed, some of it perhaps to serve as charms for good luck or placed under pillows to be slept upon and dreamt upon. The company then adjourned to the drawing room and the ballroom, and amused themselves until morning with songs, recitations, parlor-games, dances and refreshments ... The party broke up at daylight, agreeing that Mr. and Mrs. Rayner's silver wedding festival was the most enjoyable ever known in Maranoa, and wishing it would come round every year or every month. There were about twenty married ladies present, and the wit, gaiety, good looks and rich dresses they displayed were very charming. Mrs. Rayner wore silver-grey merveilleux, trimmed with plush. Miss Rayner, blue merveilleux, trimmed with cream lace ... As the sun rose the buggies began to bear away their burdens of delighted though tired guests, all wishing they might soon be inn-mates again in such an inn and for such an occasion." (1888 Silver Wedding at Hodgson [Queensland Figaro and Punch], 25 Feb 1888, p.3)

Roma vineyards—Bassett Family

1912 – "THE LATE SAMUEL BASSETT, who died at Roma last week, was born in March, 1840, at Pencorse, Summer Court, Cornwall, England. He arrived at Sydney in 1856 when 16 years of age. He was immediately engaged for a term of four years by his uncle, John Christian, Hunter River, N.S.W., where he acquired a knowledge of pastoral matters. In 1860 he came over to work on Euthilla station (10 miles from Roma), owned by his uncle, and later became manager. In 1866 he purchased 800 acres of land (now Roma Villa), and there planted the first vineyard in the Maranoa district.

In 1869 he started business in partnership with John Skinner as a general storekeeper, under the title of Bassett and Skinner. Later, in conjunction with Mr. B. F. Douglas, he acquired an interest in Mount Maria, near Morven. He also bought out Mr. Skinner's share in the storekeeping business, and appointed Mr. L. E. Johnson manager. In 1887 he sold out to the firm of Bryant and McLean, and established a depot for the sale of his wines in Roma. This he closed up in 1890. At the time of his death he had 200 acres under crop. He married in 1870 Miss Cameron, a daughter of the late John Cameron, auctioneer, of Brisbane. Deceased had been ailing for some considerable time, and the business was managed by two of the sons, William and Samuel. He leaves a widow, three daughters, and six sons." (The Late Samuel Bassett, 30 Dec 1912, p.5)

John and Harriet Keegan – Ancestry.com (Kieran_keegan84)

William and Samuel Bassett – Courtesy State Library of Queensland

Henry John Johnson – Courtesy David Johnson

William Augustus Bassett (1887-1973) managed Romavilla Winery in Roma – Courtesy State Library of Queensland

1981 THE 'LENROY' OLD SLAB HUT AT ROMA VILLA "Cottage (above) becomes Roma's first art gallery... The slab cottage, more than 90 years old, became the town's first art gallery... John Morrison and his wife Maureen opened its doors to display their wares... The Slab Cottage Gallery is set on the grounds of the equally historic Romavilla Winery, which boasts a dilapidated turn-of-the-century homestead and a functioning winery." (Sunday Mail Colour, August 5, 1984)

Top right: `Lenroy' old slab hut on right side of photo, new residential addition on left with cross veranda rails

Below right: Clark's Creek in flood, view across the creek from house site to 'Lenroy' original shearing shed and sheep yards

Below: View of 'Lenroy' old slab hut. Iron replaced the original roof; verandah enclosed for bathroom and kitchen added (structure between slab hut and tank). – Courtesy David Johnson

HOSTEL GETS SUPPORT Interestingly in 1954, "The Hostel Committee has been advised by the Johnson (Lenroy) and Aisthorpe (Mt. Abundance) families that they will each endow the hostel. This represents a donation of £1250. Advice has been received that an appeal is to be launched by the Methodist Church ... Two other well-known family groups are contemplating endowing a room. The committee advises that there are still a number of rooms that can be endowed, and they invite family groups to accept the opportunity of perpetuating their family name and tradition." (Hostel Fund Gets Stimulus, 14 Dec 1954, p.1)

While in 1928 "A peculiar accident occurred on Sunday last to a young man named Frank Trant, employed by Mr. H. Johnson, Lenroy, Dargal. A quiet bull was lying down in the yard and Trant went over to it, and sat down on the bull's back. This unusual burden startled the animal, which suddenly jumped up. The rider, in falling off, broke a bone in his leg in two places. The Ambulance was notified, and the car went out and brought the injured man in to Roma Hospital." (Roma, 27 Aug 1928, p.9)

Victor Henry Johnson, wife Ellen Rita (Nellie) Johnson (nee Wain) and son Kenneth Victor riding in sulky outside 'Lenroy' house, on Clark's Creek (June Pickering) – Ancestry.com

1924 Victor and Ellen Johnson

1947 Kenneth and Mavis Johnson
– Courtesy David Johnson

'Lenroy' original shearing shed – Courtesy David Johnson

'Lenroy' original shearing shed and sheep yards, P. D. Johnson (Doug) in the background – Courtesy David Johnson

'Lenroy' original shearing shed – Courtesy David Johnson

'Lenroy' original shearing shed, shearing – Courtesy David Johnson

'Lenroy' wool bales, Victor Henry Johnson driving Austin – Courtesy David Johnson

'Lenroy' original shearing shed, classing wool – Courtesy David Johnson

ca. 1886 B. Rayner's Royal Hotel, Hodgson (Henry John Johnson was married to Anne Benyon Rayner, Benjamin Rayner and Mary Ann Wyman's daughter) – Courtesy State Library of Queensland

'Lenroy' hay cutting – Courtesy David Johnson

Other Roma landmarks

1898 – "MR. S. S. BASSETT'S VINEYARD. A tour through the vineyards and fruit-growing areas of the district is fraught with interest, and much could be said respecting some of the well-kept and profitable holdings that I visited. Roma Vale, the property of Mr. S. S. Bassett, comprises the largest vineyard and orchard in the district. There are over 100 acres under Vines, nearly all wine-making varieties. A large and well-finished cellar, with an underground floor, is used for stocking and maturing the wines before they are offered in a marketable condition. Mr. Bassett will not allow any of his wine to leave the cellar until it is in a thoroughly sound state as regards both age and maturity. It is well got up in bottles before being sent away, and great care is directed to maintaining a retail trade.

These wines are much in favour throughout all the towns and large station properties of Western Queensland, and are now being stocked by the leading merchants along the Northern seaboard and in the Gulf country. The well-matured brands of claret, port, Madeira, and Chablis are pronounced by connoisseurs as being thoroughly sound wines, and showing little or no room for further improvement. A large orangery forms one of the important features of Mr. Bassett's estate. It has all the appearance of careful tillage, but the trees appear to have been planted almost too close together. The largest producing trees are liberally supplied with a dressing of bone manure, which is trenched in while the ground is undergoing its annual cleaning. Mr. Bassett has done much in the way of forwarding the viticultural industry of the district, and it is now pleasing to note that the excellent qualities of Australian wine which he is producing continues to meet with well-deserved appreciation." (Mr. S. S. Bassett's Vineyard, 10 Sep 1898, p.521)

1909 – ROMA VINEYARDS "If time allows a visit to the great cellars of S. S. Bassett, Roma Villa, that great pioneer of this industry ... over a glass of wine ... hear perhaps a story of industry and progress ... the early days of the Maranoa, the time of Beck and Brown, Chas. Coxen, Cobb and Co.'s coach days, and the stirring days of the opening west ... Among those firms who can be well mentioned, is that of Ballard and Crawford, coach, carriage, waggon, buggy, etc. builders, whose standard of excellence in workmanship is acknowledged from New South Wales to the Gulf, a credit which can well be extended generally to the work turned out from Roma shops. Good work is essential in the western country, and the demand has met with a willing response. At Ballard, and Crawford's a stock of upwards of 350 wheels are kept, so as to always have a well-seasoned, choice, and there, and by such attention a wide circle of the plant of trip hammers, tyre shrinkers, drilling, and other machines, lathes, band and circular saws mark the firm as being thoroughly up to date ...

In hotels the Royal may be specially mentioned as a central meeting place and most comfortable home for those away from home. Built this year the new building marks a distinct advance, and is a credit to Roma ... The coach-building works of Mr. W. Miscamble, known as the Roma Coach Works, for the 27 years of its existence has kept a name for splendid workmanship, and whether it be a new felloe, tyre, or waggon top, sulky or a Cobb's coach, the work could always be relied upon." (Roma, Western Queensland, 1 Dec 1909, p.40)

1898 – "MOUNT ABUNDANCE STATION. The only large pastoral property within easy distance of Roma is the well-known Mount Abundance station, the homestead of which is situated about five miles to the westward of the town, and which is allowed to be the best-managed and most representative pastoral property in the Maranoa district. It is a splendidly compact estate of 160,000 acres, owned by the Scottish Australian Investment Company, and composed chiefly of high, rolling, and treeless downs, the timber patches being more noticeable along the valleys of some small but dry looking watercourses, of which Bungeworgorai Creek is the principal.

The actual 'Mount Abundance,' after which the estate is named, is something over twenty miles from the homestead in a westerly direction ... As to the Mount Abundance Estate, much could be said with regard to the importance of its flocks and herds and general improvements. The homestead overlooks Bungeworgorai Creek, one of the feeders of the Balonne River, which in turn is a tributary of the Upper Darling. A splendid sheet of water has been conserved in front of the dwellings by means of an over-shot dam, constructed of basaltic cubes and concrete, which even in the severest time of drought never runs dry.

Mount Abundance house has evidently been built more with regard, for durability than for architectural effect. It is of a substantial and roomy order, with all the apartments on the one floor. The front portion of the house, which has an eastern aspect, is shaded by a wide veranda, which is further sheltered by a circular grove of picturesque and well-grown Australian bottle-trees. The surrounding buildings are sufficiently numerous to pass for a small-sized bush township, and as they include a store and saddler's and blacksmith's shops, all attended to by the employees of the company, a slight idea may be gathered from them of the great amount of labour utilised on the estate. The store is stocked with all necessaries, suitable for the every-day requirements of station employees and their families, and it is certainly one of the largest premises of its kind I have yet seen attached to any station in Queensland.

For some years the well-known Mount Abundance vineyard was worked in connection with the estate, and has obtained considerable fame for the excellent quality of wine produced. The vineyard is between twenty and thirty acres in extent, and is situated on the creek frontage, and about one mile from the homestead. Some four years ago the vineyard and cellars, inclusive of all the working plant and buildings, were leased by the S.A.I. Company to Mr. F. C. Cox, of Pimpama, who continued to produce the superior quality of wine for which Mount Abundance was so celebrated.

The principal varieties made were claret, port, and sauterne. The claret is said by connoisseur to be especially suited to the Queensland climate, being crisp, dry, and very palatable, showing a marked contrast to the heavy and full-bodied red wines offered from the Hunter River and Murray Valley districts of New South Wales.

THE ARTESIAN BORE. The Roma folk are not of an envious disposition—far from it ; but there was one matter in which they were anxious to be even with their Western neighbours, and that was with regard to an artesian water supply. For long past a permanent water supply has proved a 'burning question,' and no doubt will continue to do so until an inexhaustible supply is assured to the town. The best way in which this was calculated to be obtained was through the instrumentality of an artesian bore, and the municipality and townspeople hung on hopefully to the project, notwithstanding the strong departmental objections which were thrown in the way. It was said that the neighbourhood of Roma was outside of the cretaceous formation, and that the hope of a bore would only be accompanied by disappointment and a heavy loss. However, a bore was ultimately arranged for, and the site fixed in the height overlooking the town, so that in the event of a serviceable supply of water being struck reticulation would become an easy matter. The bore is now down to a depth of about 1700 ft., and with fair success, two or three small supplies having been struck at between 700 ft. and 1000 ft. At 1300 ft the present supply of 3500 gallons per day was obtained …

The character of the people of Western Queensland may generally be judged from the local hotels. Viewed from this stand point, Roma can be classed as one of the few meritorious centres of the West. Considering that it contains come eight or nine hostelries—a somewhat unusual number for a place of its size—the inhabitants appear to be all creditably conducted. The School of Arts and the Royal are the two hotels which cater best for the travelling public. The former was built by the late Mrs. Hogan in 1885, and is especially suited for a commercial and family trade, being well appointed with all modern requirements." (The Sketcher, 10 Sep 1898, p.519)

Royal Hotel

1870 – "ROMA. Cook's Royal Hotel had a narrow escape from destruction by fire on the morning of Monday last. A young man, having to leave early, whilst dressing perceived a light in a room at some distance; but thought it was some one else dressing by the light of a candle—the partitions dividing the rooms do not reach the roof, so that a light can be seen from one room to another ; however, on leaving his room, he smelt fire ; hearing a crackling, opened the door, and perceived the bed and some of the wood work ignited. He immediately gave the alarm, and, assistance being at hand, the fire was extinguished. I suppose about £20 will be the extent of the damage done. The only way they have to account for its origin is the fact that a gentleman, who had previously occupied the room, but had left, returned between 10 and 11 o'clock the previous night, and had taken a candle in order to get some article he had left behind ; and it is supposed that some sparks from the candle, or from his pipe, had fallen on the bed, as it was evident from the blankets and palliasse that it had been smouldering for some time." (Roma, 12 Oct 1870, p.3)

1915 – "FIRE IN ROMA. Royal Hotel Burned. The Commissioner of Police has been advised that a fire occurred in Roma at about half-past 2 o'clock this morning, resulting in the destruction of the Royal Hotel, one of the principal hotels in the town, and 10 small shops in the same block in the main street. Adjacent to the destroyed buildings are the new shops and offices erected by the Roma Town Council. The Royal Hotel was a large new two-storied wooden building. The fire started in the hotel, but the cause has not been ascertained." (Fire in Roma, 10 May 1915, p.2)

1917 – "BLAZE AT ROMA. Royal Hotel Destroyed. Roma. Friday. One of the most imposing structures in Roma, the Royal Hotel, was, with the contents, completely destroyed by fire shortly before 2 o'clock this morning. This is the second occasion on which the hotel has been destroyed. The fire, so far as can be gathered, started in an unoccupied bedroom, and spread with remarkable rapidity, not-withstanding the fact that the hotel was constructed of brick … The Royal Hotel was … occupied by Mr. H. H. Humphrey, and owned by Mrs. R. Winten … The hotel had only been re-erected 12 months ago last September … The Royal was regarded as one of the finest hotels outside the metropolis." (Blaze at Roma, 15 Dec 1917, p.4)

1919 – "FIRE AT ROMA. Royal Hotel Destroyed. Roma, Monday.—The Royal Hotel, a large one-story building, was destroyed by fire early this morning. The cause of the outbreak is unknown." (Fire at Roma, 11 Mar 1919, p.4)

1931 – "BLAZE AT ROMA. Seven Buildings Destroyed. BRISBANE, Jan. 2.— Damage estimated at £7,000 was caused by a fire which, early this morning, at Roma, destroyed the Royal Mail Hotel, Hunter's store, the Post Office, a billiard saloon, a fruit shop, a baker's shop and a dwelling." (Blaze at Roma, 3 Jan 1931, p.6)

1938 – "TWO FIRES IN ROMA … While the Fire Brigade were still engaged extinguishing the flames, the fire alarm again sounded, and they again quickly responded. The scene of the second fire was a boarding house at the rear of the Royal Hotel in Hawthorne-street, owned by Mr. J. McMullen. The building had not been occupied for a considerable time. The fire was discovered in a corner of one of the rooms, but although some of the boards were burnt the flames were extinguished before any considerable damage had occurred." (Two Fires in Roma, 23 Mar 1938, p.2)

ca. 1890s S.S. Bassetts Vineyard, Roma – Courtesy The University of Queensland

Homestead at Bassetts Romavilla Winery, Roma – Courtesy State Library of Queensland

10 May 1915 Charred remains of the Royal Hotel, Roma – Courtesy State Library of Queensland

10 May 1915 Royal Hotel in Roma on fire – Courtesy State Library of Queensland

Pre-1917 Royal Hotel, Roma – Courtesy Flickr

ca. 1910 Drafting yards at Mt. Abundance – Courtesy State Library of Queensland

Early 1900s Roma Hospital – Courtesy Flickr

1920 Court House, Roma – Courtesy Flickr

Lingley's Hotel Muckadilla – Courtesy State Library of Queensland

1903 Royal Hotel at Morven – Courtesy State Library of Queensland

Chapter Seven

Charleville-a coach building town

COBB AND CO.

By Will H. Ogilvie

By north and south, and east and west;
By dawn and dark of day;
By swamps and plains and mountain crest
They take the foremost way.
And where the slanting sunrays dip,
And underneath the stars,
Is heard the thunder of the whip
And creaking of the barn;
And out beyond the reach of rail,
As far as wheel-tracks go,
The drovers round their campfire hail
The lights of Cobb and Co.

(Cobb and Co., Verse 1, 20 Apr 1895, p.9)

The Never Never

"It is now many years since the early pioneers of western Queensland knocked together the first humpy on the bank of the Warrego River, 483 miles west of Brisbane, where now stands Charleville—one of Queensland's premier inland towns. At that time, this locality was viewed from more populous districts as bordering upon the

'Never Never' of the interior.

With the advance of enterprise and settlement, however, the country gradually developed into one of the finest pastoral areas of the colony, possessing a population of 3,211 souls. The town's population was recorded as 1,456 in the census of 1891. From its foundation, Charleville has been a thriving community, but its progress became most marked after it became the terminal town of the western railway in 1888 ...

The bore is the only 'lion' Charleville may be said to possess, but it is a worthy monument to Nature's generosity, forethought, and the science of the age ... From the open shaft, the water attains a height of 45 ft, and this is increased to 150 ft by the application of a 5-inch nozzle. The spectacle of the water in action is a most brilliant one. During the bush strike of 1891, a bathhouse with the necessary fittings was erected at the bore ... A refreshing bathe may now be indulged in for the modest fee of 2d." (The Sketcher, 30 Jun 1894, p.1319)

Trip—Charleville to Dalby

1876 "CHARLEVILLE TO DALBY per Cobb and Co.'s Coach. On a bright January morning, 1876—well, to be precise, it was on a Sunday morning, the 2nd January, 1876, that the celebrated Cobb and Co. started their first coach from the fair city of Charleville to that equally as fair city Roma."

Bradley's farm, dam mail-station horse change, 'tank'

"At 7.20 the well-known cry of 'All aboard' sounded on the sweet morning air, when your humble servant having taken his seat, together with A. Broomfield (the driver that is to be) and Jerry Murphy of happy memory, who handled the ribbons on this auspicious occasion, started away with a spanking team of four horses, which Jerry tooled along at 'knots' an hour, the country looking black, dry, and parched, and no grass. Made Bradley's farm at 9.20, and got to the dam mail-station at 10.12, where we had the first change of horses. This time Broomfield took them in hand, and away again over parched, and grassless country. The fine clear morning air having sharpened our appetites, we had recourse to a goodly-sized package of sandwiches and a small 'wee drap' out of the flask, and we all felt considerably better. (I may here state that it is necessary for passengers to take a little refreshment with them, as at present there is no accommodation on the road until you reach Maryvale.) Pulled up, and watered the horses at the 'tank,' where Murphy intends having a mail-station; away again, the horses much refreshed after imbibing. It was now we began to feel the heat : it was like a furnace. I may say that I felt as hot as two furnaces : about 140° in the sun. It was now that our water-bags came into action. I can tell you that a drink of cold water in a waterless bush, under a blazing January sun, is a luxury not to be thought too lightly of ;

and the man that invented water bags ought to have a front seat in heaven."

Humbug Creek horse change, Maryvale horse change

"It was just 3.15 when we pulled up at J. Reid's Humbug Creek. Jerry here traded in horses, bought three, and broke-in one in about five minutes. Away on again, the horse broke-in going as if it had been used to it all its life; on, still on, over parched country. Hot : why hot is no name for it : it felt just as if the silver was up to 375° instead of 140°. At 6.30 we made Leadbetter's (Maryvale) ; our first day's stage, and our sleeping place for the night. Your humble servant was only too glad to get a nice cool wash, and, not forgetting the inner man, we all sat down to a good comfortable meal, Mr. Leadbetter and his amiable daughter attending to our wants ; and then, with pipe in mouth, we stretched ourselves on the verandah to enjoy the evening breeze. I managed to secure a couch that was kindly brought on to the verandah by Mrs. Leadbetter, and there slept comfortably through the night, the soft cool morning air sweeping o'er me. I awoke at the sound of Jerry's voice asking me if I intended sleeping all day. Referring to my Boston lever, I found it had registered 5 o'clock. Jumped out of bed, had a refreshing wash, and was ready for breakfast. That meal finished, Jerry bought, and broke-in a very fine horse. (Jerry is pretty smart at anything.) Off again at 6 o'clock on the 3rd instant, bowling along at a slapping pace. No grass ; everything dry as dust."

Victoria Downs horse change, Black's Waterholes horse change, Moor Creek horse change, Womballala

"Pulled up at Victoria Downs (Sadlier's Waterholes) ; changed horses at Corbett's, where the usual amount of 'bar-loafers' with bloated faces, in a dreary state, were knocking around ; hitched up, and away by 7.30. Soon after passed the up horse-mail (Cobb and Co.) going at a 'good bat.' Saw a few mangy paddy melons. I had rather they, had been watermelons : I could have done better with them. Arrived at Black's Waterholes ; pulled up at the Traveller's Best Hotel; kept by J. M'Kenzie, just at 10 a.m. where we had a good comfortable lunch properly cooked and placed upon the table as it ought to be—a thing rather unusual in road-side houses. I can recommend this house to 'all whom it may concern'—all travellers who study comfort, and the good things of this life. Off again, with a change of horses, at 11 a.m. Slid along merrily. Still over parched and grassless country. The water bag—the grandest institution in Queensland : 'can't be licked'—came into requisition every now and then. Changed horses at Moor Creek and away again by 1 o'clock.

Went through some performance at Womballala, where there is a nice waterhole, but failing fast : rain wanted badly to keep up the supply. Heavy thunderstorm working up in the south-west ; just got on the black-soil plains when it commenced blowing a hurricane."

Mitchell Downs horse change, Amby Downs mail station and horse change, Muckadilla horse change

"Put the horses along—well, a locomotive would have no show with us ; ran into Mitchell Downs, delivered mails, and drew up at Sam Stewart's. Came on to rain ; had a wash, but in water I dare be sworn that if a thermometer had been plunged into it it would have sent the silver up to 102°. I suggested to the buxom waiting-maid to get some water from the water-bag hanging in the verandah, when she exclaimed, *What! for the bedrooms*, evidently looking on the contents of a water-bag as sacred to drinking purposes ; had a good square meal, and retired. At about 3 o'clock was awoke by the music of pigs and dogs. Sam must think more of them than his lodgers : one night is ample. Up at 6 o'clock, washed in water somewhat cooler than the previous night ; had breakfast, all aboard at 7 o'clock on the 4th instant, made tracks for Amby Downs, and crossed the Maranoa River—that is, it would have been a river had there been any water. The rain the night previous made the blacksoil plains rather heavy, had to take out the break block. Rolled along to Amby Downs mail station, which was reached at 10 o'clock, and changed horses. On, still on! Away to Muckadilla, Jerry putting the coach through. Arrived there at 12 o'clock ; had a wash and dinner.

Lots of carriers camped. Fresh horses hitched up, all aboard, and away over the everlasting parched-up country."

Bindango mail station and horse change, Roma horse change

"Arrived at Bindango at 2 p.m.—mail-station. No groom or horses in sight; we all thought it a case of 'jam pickled stale,' when suddenly a Deitcher groom—who is a makeshift, the one appointed being away, having had the misfortune to lose his wife—put in an appearance, and on seeing him Jerry sung out, *Where are the horses?* when Herr Von Klingindricker (I believe that's his name ; if not, it was equally as long) said in answer, *I wast told dat de horses was to be mit de yard, bis four de clock*. Having informed Jerry that the horses were 'down the creek,' the groom was started off after them, and kept us waiting—well, close up two hours. Once more aboard. On, on ! over plains ; no fine open plains or well-grassed downs greeted our sight—nothing but the everlasting dry parched-up country. Storm brewing in the south-east. Ran into Roma, and delivered the mails at 5.30 p.m., thus doing the journey comfortably in three days. On the 5th instant left Roma at 9 p.m. in well, I cannot dignify it with the name of a coach: it's something of a cross between a Melbourne car and a wheelbarrow ; the reverse of comfortable to ride in, and badly horsed—only had two in where four actually wanted, but we managed to 'work our passage' until met (luckily) by Cobb's groom with a spare horse, which was hitched in the lead. The driver also pressed the horse the groom was riding into the service, and placed him in the 'wheel,' the one whose place he filled being 'regularly baked,' and no doubt was thankful for the change."

Blythdale horse change, Pickenjenny, Wallumbilla

"Got to Blythdale at 11.15, the country looking bare of grass. Changed horses—three this time, and wanted. Off again on very bad roads, and got to the creek luxuriating in the euphonious title of 'Pickenjenny' at 1.20, where we dined in—well, a house sent into this breathing world scarce half made up.

The floors, walls, windows, and doors will no doubt grow in time.

Got through with the dinner. All aboard, and, after having a rough time of it, pulled up at Wallumbilla, my Waltham lever showing 3.15. Off once more ; very hot. Storm out south ; electric fluid very lively ; distant thunder very audible."

Euleba

"Arrived at Euleba at 6.30 : a very long and tedious stage of sixteen miles—about the worst sixteen miles of bad roads I wish to travel over, and I have not the slightest doubt that if the three poor horses who were unfortunate enough to be hitched to the before-mentioned 'hybrid' vehicle were capable, they would endorse my opinion. Nothing but stony and sandy spinifex ridges. As before-mentioned, we got to Euleba, and pulled up at the hotel bearing that name kept by mine host Winieke, the verandah of which was in possession of travellers, the ground around being strewn with the everlasting concomitant of travellers on horse and foot— viz., pack-saddles and bags, hobbles, 'jackshays' neatly rolled top, blankets, and the never-to-be-forgotten billy and water-bag. The up-coach from Dalby having arrived we all had tea, when, as usual, hot meat was served on cold plates. This cold-plate arrangement applies to all the hotels visited along the line—a thing, if altered, no doubt travellers would be thankful. Around Euleba it looks fresh and green ; they have a splendid waterhole. I forgot to mention we had a passenger from Roma to Euleba : the Roma ex-bellman and crier—an amusing 'cuss'—who made us acquainted with all the Roma scandal in a very short time, not forgetting the secrets of the new Order of Brighamism. Left Euleba at 'sun up' on the 6th instant; over sandy country made hard by the previous night's rain, everything looking green, and nice grass."

Tchanning Creek, Moraby, Stockyard horse change, Condamine horse change

"Arrived at the Tchanning Creek at 7 o'clock; had breakfast—a nice clean comfortable breakfast. On, still on again!

Arrived at Moraby at 11 o'clock ; had dinner and a good feed of grapes. Off again ; changed horses at 'stockyard.' Still onwards! Country rangy ; here and there belts of scrub, patches of open grass land. Arrived at the Condamine at 4 p.m. ; awfully dull place—would take about two earthquakes to wake it up. Left Condamine at 4 a.m. on the 7th instant—dark, cold, half-asleep. Got to the 12 mile at 6.15 ; had breakfast, changed horses, and off."

WOMBA MAIL STATION AND HORSE CHANGE, WOMBA 10-MILE, KOGAN, DAANDINE, DALBY

"Arrived at Womba mail-station at 8 o'clock ; another change, and still going. Good grass all the way; lot of wool-teams camped here. Got to the Womba 10-mile at 10 a.m. A very dangerous bridge to cross; wants hand-rails or chain. If the leader took it into his head to be lively, might fly off at a tangent, which might be awkward for those aboard. Good grass about here ; would gladden the hearts of the Warrego squatters had they the like. Changed, and away. Dined at the Kogan. Away to the Daandine, the Bridge, and finally pulled up at the Royal Hotel, Dalby, at 6.25 ; and thus parted with Cobb and Co.'s coach for the one drawn by the iron horse." (Charleville to Dalby per Cobb and Co.'s Coach., 22 Jan 1876, p.3) See *Appendix 7.1 Postal Directory Examples*

Charleville

1879 – COACH STUCKUP "Oct. 20.— Roma to Charleville coach stuckup by an armed man named John Haslin. Constable Pettit, who was on the box, arrested the man, and was awarded a gratuity of £20. Haslin got 10 years." (Queensland's Half Century 1859 to 1909 Notable Events, 8 Dec 1909, pp.23-37)

1890 – FLOODS "Charleville, February 20. Thick steady rain set in yesterday morning, with an east south east wind. Since then about 2 in of rain have fallen, and the Warrego River is higher than at any period since the big flood of 1890. The river is still rising and sweeping round the billabongs, and a heavy flood is expected. The barometer has fallen considerably during the afternoon, and rain is still falling. The Cunnamulla coach, which arrived sixteen hours late to day brings news of heavy rain and rising floods all along the road. At Augathella the Warrego is a banker and still rising ; 2in. of rain have fallen since Monday. The Blackall coach has been detained here since Sunday. To the westward Langlo and Blackwater rivers are in flood, and traffic is at a standstill throughout the district. Cobb and Co's agent has wired to Brisbane not to book any passengers. There is every prospect of a splendid winter, and so far there has been general rejoicing at the general appearance of the rain." (Weather and Stock Movements, 21 Feb 1890, p.5)

1890 – "COACH BOGGED During the heavy floods in January last one of Cobb and Co.'s coaches got bogged at Long Creek between Charleville and Adavale. The vehicle was recovered last Saturday in a very dilapidated condition." (The Brisbane Courier, 28 Nov 1890, p.4)

1892 – "STOCK PASSINGS : On the 26th October, 10,320 sheep, from Burrenbilla to Gallagher's selection, near Charleville, Cobb and Co. owners, J. Clair in charge." (Stock Movements and State of the Country, 5 Nov 1892, p.905)

CHARLEVILLE COACH FACTORY

In 1897, Cobb and Co. shared their experience in vehicle manufacturing. "A short sketch of our history in connection with the manufacture of high-class road vehicles will no doubt interest you. We started manufacturing in Brisbane in the early 1860s for our own Coaching Business and the public generally. The great experience gained by actually using our own made traps for our own work will be readily seen and appreciated by you. We were able to personally and thoroughly test and prove every new design of construction, variety of timber, quality of paint and other material, and sift out all that were found wanting before introducing them in traps for the public. As our coach routes extended out West we commenced to notice

that our vehicles built with the coastal seasoned timbers would not stand the dry inland climate, they would crack and gape at all joints.

This became so serious at last that we decided to move our Factory to a suitable inland locality, and after considerable thought Charleville, nearly 500 miles inland, was chosen, and our whole plant and equipment moved to there in 1886. We had another Factory in Bathurst, N.S.W., and the machinery and plant from there were also removed to Charleville at the same time, making jointly a substantial and up-to-date plant and a greatly increased staff of expert workmen. The effect of this move was immediately apparent, for we purchased large stocks of timber and seasoned it in the same hot dry climate in which traps when built were used, and the result proved extremely satisfactory. We still carry big stocks of timber to make sure that only thoroughly seasoned wood gets into the vehicles, and that is why coastal built traps cannot compete with our inland seasoned make for lasting and enduring qualities. We have profited considerably by our over half a century's experiences, and are able to give you the full benefit of those experiences in any work you entrust to us. We feel sure we are able to give you a vehicle at a price as reasonable as one landed from a coastal builder, with the added advantages of containing thoroughly seasoned timber and being built with a full knowledge of the work required of it. We maintain it pays to buy the best ... Yours faithfully, Cobb & Co. Ltd." (Cobb & Co.'s Catalogue of High Class Vehicles, 1897)

But later that same year, disaster struck. "At about 2 o clock this morning a fire broke out in Cobb and Co's large coach factory. The buildings and the whole of the contents were totally destroyed in a very short time nothing being saved. In the building, besides the expensive machinery, were a large number of buggies and two new coaches, also some vehicles belonging to townspeople.

Thirty regular hands were employed in the establishment besides others. These men are consequently thrown out of work. This factory was by far the most complete and extensive of the kind in Queensland. The property, as far as is known, was insured in the New Zealand Insurance Company for a little over £3,000, and the loss is estimated at considerably over £10,000." (Fire at Charleville, 17 Nov 1897, p.5)

Despite the setback, Cobb and Co. continued to innovate. In 1901, they completed a major project. "Messrs. Cobb and Co., have just finished at their Charleville factory the largest coach ever constructed by them. The wheels are 4ft. and 5ft. in diameter with tires 4 inches wide, and bevelled felloes. The body is an extra large one with three seats capable of seating 12 persons. The centre seat lifts up, so that a passenger may pass to the back seat without inconvenience. Two side doors are also fitted to the coach and the seats are well padded with cushions, and the sides of the coach with squabs. The entire length of the vehicle is 13 feet, and the top is capable of carrying a great deal of luggage. The coach is a very roomy one, and has been constructed for heavy passenger traffic in the Hughenden district. This is the first broad-tyred coach ever built, and in sandy or flat country will no doubt prove a decided success. Messrs. Cobb and Co. are to be complimented on their enterprise. —Times." (A Large Coach, 12 Aug 1901, p.2)

By 1920, however, the era of coaching was coming to an end. "After 60 years manufacturing, Cobb and Co. notify by advertisement that they intend to dispose of their large coach and buggy factory at Charleville. The factory, in the first instance, was built to turn out suitable coaches and light vehicles for the numerous mail contracts, but now that most of these have been relinquished, the necessity for the factory has disappeared.

It is intended to dispose of the factory as a going concern, or to sell the stock, plant, and freehold separately to suit various buyers." (Cobb and Co.'s Charleville Factory, 26 Nov 1920, p.4)

The closure was felt deeply in the community. "Charleville, December 18. Much regret was expressed here at the closing down of Cobb and Co.'s large factory to-day, which is a distinct loss to the town and district, besides causing the unemployment of several workmen." (Cobb & Co.'s Coach Factory, 25 Dec 1920, p.16)

And so, the doors finally closed. "COBB AND COMPANY. The Western Santa Claus. Charleville, Monday. The finest sight for a long time was witnessed here, when Messrs. Cobb and Co., Ltd., sent out their special coach to rural districts,

loaded with Christmas boxes and Christmas cakes.

The children gave a bright, hearty laugh when, the driver pulled up at the respective destinations. The driver heard much to cheer his own heart, such remarks being passed as, 'That's from Granny in Brisbane!' 'That's from Uncle Tom at Toowoomba!' and so on. Cobb's factory, which has been open for nearly 30 years, closed its doors, once and for all, on Sunday last." (Cobb and Company, 21 Dec 1920, p.5)

Aerial Mail

In 1922, a new era of communication began with the introduction of aerial mail. "The Deputy Postmaster-General, Mr. McConachie advises that the tentative time-table for the aerial mail service between Charleville and Cloncurry has been arranged. The service will commence shortly. Only first class mail matter, that is letters, post cards, and letter cards, will be carried. The mail must be specifically endorsed and each missive must bear in postage stamps a special fee of 3d. for each half-ounce or portion thereof in addition to the ordinary rate of postage.

It is proposed that the mail shall leave Charleville on Thursday mornings at 6.30, calling at Tambo, Blackall, Longreach, Winton, and Mackinlay, and will reach Cloncurry at 12.20 p.m. on Friday. A departure will be taken from Cloncurry at 6.30 a.m. on Sunday and the mail will reach Charleville, after calling at the same towns as on the forward journey, at 11.40 a.m. on Monday." (Aerial Mail, 14 Oct 1922, p.44)

Later that year, the demand for air travel was already growing with a "BIGGER PLANE NEEDED. Quite a large number ... were present at the aerial depot yesterday to witness the arrival of the aerial mail from Cloncurry and Winton. The machine reached here on scheduled time.

The pilot regretfully had to leave a number of passengers behind ...

a big plane is expected to arrive from London in February next." (Aerial Mail, 27 Dec 1922, p.2)

By 1929, air travel had become a practical option for business. "AN AERIAL TRIP, with plenty of time for business at Dalby and Roma ... 11 hours from the time of departure from Brisbane to return. Roma is distant 315 miles from Brisbane by rail, and the time taken by the Western mail train is 14 hours in each direction." (Aerial Business Trip to Roma, 30 Jan 1929, p.17)

Meanwhile, 1922 also marked the symbolic end of an era. "With the final passing of Cobb and Co. at the end of 1921 another link with the old days has snapped. On January 10, F. Palmer, mail contractor, between Charleville and Tambo (Queensland) took over the remaining plant of Cobb and Co." (Cobb and Co., 9 Feb 1922, p. 4.)

ca. 1873 Arrival of Cobb's coach at post office, Clermont, Queensland (Richard James Cottell)
– Courtesy National Library of Australia

Factory at Charleville – Cobb & Co.'s Catalogue of High Class Vehicles, p.102

ca. 1895 Cobb and Co. coach at Railway Station in Charleville – Courtesy State Library of Queensland

ca. 1912 People in the street outside the post office in Alfred Street, Charleville – Courtesy State Library of Queensland

ca. 1890 Mail coach pulled up outside the Charleville Hotel – Courtesy State Library of Queensland

ca. 1909 Cobb & Co. stables, Galatea Street, Charleville – Courtesy State Library of Queensland

ca. 1906 Cobb and Co. mail coach at Charleville, Steve Wall driving – Courtesy State Library of Queensland

1902-1904 Charleville Hotel (George Balsillie) – Courtesy State Library of Queensland

ca. 1902 Charleville Brewery (George Balsillie) – Courtesy State Library of Queensland

ca. 1880-1890 Charleville branch of the Commercial Bank in Western Queensland – Courtesy State Library of Queensland

Chapter Eight

Beyond Charleville

COBB AND CO.
By Will H. Ogilvie

The settlers wait at death of day
To hear their rolling wheels,
Where faintly through the twilight grey
The far whip challenge steals;
They take the messages of love
And bring them safely through—
The faithful sun that rides above
Is not more loyal true—
They bear the lines of shame and sin,
The words of weal and woe;
And life itself is trusted in
The hands of Cobb and Co.

(Cobb and Co., Verse 2, 20 Apr 1895 , p.9)

Queensland Cobb and Co.

"The first Queensland Cobb and Co., Limited, was incorporated in August, 1881. The capital was £50,000 in 500 shares of £100 each, of which 300 were then issued fully paid up, the balance being held by the Company for further issue. The shareholders then registered held the following value in shares:—W. R. Hall (Sydney), £9,000; J. Rutherford (Bathurst), £10,000; F. Shaw (Brisbane), £2,000; I. T. Bartholomew (Goganga) grazier, £1,000; T. Gallagher (St. George), £600; C. M. Kirk (St. George), £1,000; F. C. Shaw (Bogantungan), £1,000; H. W. Shaw (Emerald), £900; H. B. Taylor (Tambo), £1,000; R. McMaster (Aramac), £400; J. Coyle (Roma) £200; W. J. Richardson (St. George) £200; L. Uhl, saddler (Brisbane), £200; J. Coyle (Charters Towers), £1,000; W. Jenkins (Mangalore), grazier, £100; John Bock (Cunnamulla), £400 ... under the governing director, Mr. Rutherford ...

Lines included St. George and district to Thargomindah, via Bollon, Cunnamulla, Mitchell, and up the Balonne to Surat and Yeulba; Roma to Charleville, via Mitchell and Morven; Charleville to Adavale, via the Ward and Langlo; Cunnamulla, via Dynevor Downs to Thargomindah; Cunnamulla, down the Warrego to Barringun, New South Wales; Charleville to Augathella, Tambo, and Blackall line; Westwood in the early 70s [1870s] to Clermont; Blackall to Withersfield; Comet to Springsure; Aramac and Muttaburra; Winton to Cork Station; Muttaburra to Longreach; Winton and Boulia via 20-mile Hotel, Western Hotel, Elderslie, Woodstock, Llanheidol, Warenda, Boulia, Bourke; Winton, Ayrshire Downs, Dagworth, Kynuna; Winton, Oondooroo, Corfield, Stamford, Hughenden; Hughenden, Marathon, Richmond, Neila Ponds, Eddington, Leile Vale, Cloncurry." (Coaching in Australia a history of the coaching firm Cobb and Co., W. Lees, 1917, p.41)

"Agencies and Agents at: Augathella (J. Campbell), Bollon (A. Brettell), Charleville (C. E. Search), Cunnamulla (W. H. Tuite), Eulo (P. R. Beresford), Jundah (L. Stephenson), Longreach (G. Riddell), Mitchell (Hammonds), Mungindi (A. Irwin), St. George (E. Gallagher), Surat (E. J. Simpson), Tambo (G. H. Brown), Thallon (F. Mcloughlin), Thargomindah (R. Speedy), Winton (R. Swan), Yeulba (A. Senyard)." (Coaching in Australia a history of the coaching firm Cobb and Co., W. Lees, 1917)

A trip from from Brisbane to Adavale

In 1886, a travelling correspondent described a journey from Brisbane to Adavale with vivid detail. "Having booked seats at Cobb and Co.'s office, in Brisbane, for coach from a place bearing the name of Dulbydilla to Adavale, a party of five jovial spirits life by tram on a Friday afternoon for Ipswich, which sleepy town was reached in due time. Next morning we embarked on the mail train from the metropolis, as it lay pulling and panting, at the Ipswich station, and set forth on the monotonous journey to the West. Beyond a discussion as to the beauty of the range scenery compared with that of the Blue Mountains in New South Wales, the tree-clad mountains and gaping ravines we passed through attracted but little attention.

On arrival at Toowoomba the station, as usual, was crowded with more sightseers than expectant friends. Of all the stations on the Southern and Western line for Toowoomba takes the palm for being thronged on the arrival of each train with a number of persons whose only object appears to stare travellers out of countenance. After doing ample justice to the refreshments dispensed by Host Higgins, we set out for Dalby rushing over the undulating downs dotted with sheep calmly browsing the luxurious and plentiful grass. Here and there a giddy goat could be seen frisking merrily, unabashed by the presence and venerable aspect of the bearded leader.

But all these were left behind and Dalby was reached, looking dull and burned up in the blazing sunlight. Without wishing to hurt the susceptibilities of the Dalbyites, I must say their town as seen from the station appeared as if some wag of a genius had, in a moment of merriment, ascended the empyrean and shaken down with a niggard hand a number of galvanised iron roofs. At the station one can get a fair square feed in the dining room, or can munch a sandwich, washed down with a glass of queer colonial, at the counter. In time Dalby was left behind, as was station after station until Miles was stopped at. It was Saturday evening, and a number of people (perhaps the population of Miles) were sitting on their haunches on the rails. They were all bedight in their best, consisting chiefly of moleskins, bluchers, crimean shirts, felt or cabbage-tree, and the eternal white neckerchief. They looked on, gasped, and never said a word, and if they had been glued to the rails they could not have been more motionless.

After a hearty meal at Miles we set out for Roma and when that place was reached there was a bustling and babbling crowd on the platform. A rain-like haze obscured the moon, and nothing but the gleaming lights could be seen of the town. Ten or twenty minutes were allowed here for the passengers to stretch their legs 'ashore.' The ride to Dulbydilla was a dreary one. Closing the windows to keep the cold night air out, and wrapping the rugs around us, we all soon fell into a dreamy dose, or a succession of dreamy doses each of which was only of short duration. Every time one awoke it was only to hear the puffing and the straining of the engine and the creaking of the carriages, and looking out of the window, the trees could be seen flying past, as it were, like a phalanx of phantoms in the magical moonlight.

At last, about 2 o'clock in the morning, the word 'Dulbydilla' was sounded in our ears, and feeling cold, sleepy, and miserable, we set out for the hotel at a distance of a few hundred yards, leaving the luggage to follow in the care of a gloomy and silent gentlemen in a possum skin cap. It must be said the aspect of affairs at the hotel was uninviting and cheerless. There was no fire blaming on the hearth at which we might thaw five frozen bodies, there was no steaming and tempting meal, such as Dickens and Washington Irving were never tired of serving up. Everybody appeared to be wrapped up in himself, and all moved about like spectres.

About an hour after arrival a cold collation was served up, and as if infected by the gloom that overhung everything, we sat down and silently and solemnly ate the corned and roast beef before us.

The coach office is attached to the hotel, and the clerk is a quiet and methodical little man of business. His office was rendered cheerful and comfortable by a fire brightly burning in a little stove, and he kindly invited us in, and presented us with a late number of the Saturday Review, which proved most acceptable. About 4 o'clock, the cheery voice of Alf Bloomfield, the coachman, was heard lustily shouting 'all aboard', and mounting the box seat with a friend we dashed out of Dulbydilla at a fine pace behind six beautiful dapple-grays (Cobb's best) and over two tons weight on the coach.

The air at this time was not very cold, but crisp and delightful and the moon,

Like a globe of silver hung straight before us, simmering gently on the tree tops, and lighting up the avenues through which we dashed.

Wrapped in our overcoats and mufflers, and bound round with rugs, a gentle glow suffused our bodies, and the drive proved most enjoyable. Bloomfield, as a driver, is one not easily surpassed. The manner in which he tooled the six splendid animals round trees and stumps, over logs ruts, and stones, went far to confirm us in the generally expressed opinion that he is one of the best drivers King Cobb has in his employ.

On the road we passed numerous teams, some laden with wool, others with produce, and the flames from the camp fires flickered and fell, casting grotesque shadows that danced among the trees weirdly. But the moon soon disappeared, and the ghostly dawn with its grim light came in succession, bringing with it a keen cold that made the flesh on one's face tingle. And when the great golden sun arose a pleasant warmth was quickly diffused among the chattering and shivering travellers, and later on beads of perspiration stood on the foreheads of those on the box.

The light of day, however, displayed a saddening panorama. Nothing before us but a dreary stretch of road, nothing on each side but barren ground as bare as a beach as far as grass was concerned, and covered with the mournful murmuring mulga-tree. Past this ground, past fostering cattle and bleachening bones, past poor thin and worn looking cattle, with a sky of brass overhead, and burning, blazing sun still on the patient animals, drew us until night fell, and again the moon rose

With a mysterious splendour Touching the sombre leaves.

Still on we flew, and after 8 o'clock darted up the wide street of Charleville. The air of this township is most salubrious, it is mild and dry, and fills the lungs to their utmost extent, until one feels the chest expanding under its influence. Before daybreak next morning (Monday), we were again on the coach, passing through the same dreary country, past the mulga cut down for the cattle to eat, post more dead animals, past places, misnamed rivers and without a drop of water in them, and still on we went until we reached a place called the 'Camps,' where a roaring fire was awaiting us and a hot supper. After this we camped in comfortable beds in the tents, and early next morning set out in the coach, when again miles, of weary miles were passed over such country as previously described, and night sank and we arrived at Adavale about 8 o'clock. Of Adavale there will be more to be said anon for the present it only remains to be said that the people of Brisbane have no idea of the awful state of the country that is passed through from Dulbydilla to here.

The ground is bare, and without a blade or even the roots of grass. It is nothing but heartrending stretches of sand, covered with mulga, coolabah and other unsightly trees. Of the mulga it must be said that the cattle eat it greedily, and it is their only means of subsistence in the localities where it grows. The few inches of rain that have fallen lately have had no effect whatever beyond supplying sheets of water that are rapidly evaporating. It would appear that nothing but a heavy deluge would again give the ground its garb of verdure and if such does not quickly come, God help the squatter is the fervent prayer of those who have passed through this deplorable country. As a young squatter solemnly remarked, as he cast his eye over this terrible land, as he sat on the coach, It seemed as if the Creator had cursed the country. And so it would seem, and let us all hope that before long the wretched land will be

Made green with the running of rivers.

(From Brisbane to Adavale, 3 May 1886, p.6)

COACHING SERVICE 1878—"Cobb & Co.'s Telegraph Line of Royal Mail Coaches Head Office : Albert-street. Brisbane to Sandgate; Sandgate to Brisbane; Gympie to Maryborough; Maryborough to Gympie; Brisbane to Gympie; Gympie to Brisbane; Brisbane to Beenleigh; Beenleigh to Brisbane; Brisbane to Pimpama and Nerang Creek; Nerang Creek and Pimpama to Brisbane; Warwick to Tenterfield; Tenterfield to Maryland and Warwick; Warwick to Stanthorpe; Stanthorpe to Warwick; Stanthorpe to Wilson's Downfall; Wilson's Downfall to Stanthorpe; Chinchilla to Roma; Roma to Chinchilla; Roma to Charleville; Charleville to Roma; Townsville to Charters Towers and Ravenswood; Ravenswood to Charters Towers and Townsville; Charters Towers to Townsville and Ravenswood; Blackwater to Clermont and Copperfield; Copperfield and Clermont to Blackwater; Blackwater to Springsure; Springsure to Blackwater ... FREDK. SHAW, Manager." (Classified Advertising, 8 Nov 1878, p.4)

Those were the days

"Those were the days, 'pulsating with life and brimful of laughter'—those were grand, brave generous days of Cobb and Co.! …Wayside Eating House … There was something stimulating in an early morning ride behind a team, fresh from the last mail change. On we went, the crisp breeze in our faces sharpening our appetites for a mid-day meal at the next shanty. *Gents, what'll you 'ave was the greeting of mine host. There's lamb, ram, sheep and mutton* … With the passing of Cobb and Co. closed one of the most picturesque and romantic chapters in our country's history." (The Roaring Days, 17 Jun 1926, p.15) ca. 1911 Cobb and Co. coach and others in front of the Adavale Post Office – Courtesy State Library of Queensland

Cobb & Co. coach at the Nive Hotel – Courtesy State Library of Queensland

ca. 1910 Activity around the entrance to Nive Downs Station, Augathella – Courtesy State Library of Queensland

ca. 1920 Cobb & Co. coach in front of the Cloncurry Post & Telegraph Office – Courtesy State Library of Queensland

ca. 1907 Mail coaches leaving Cloncurry (The Crown Studios) – Courtesy State Library of Queensland

ca. 1914 Cobb & Co. stagecoach outside a building at Nive Downs Station – Courtesy State Library of Queensland

ca. 1910 Crossing the bridge over the Comet River, Carnarvon District – Courtesy State Library of Queensland

1922 Cobb & Co. coach on the last trip between Longreach and Jundah (S. C. Kerr) – Courtesy State Library of Queensland

ca. 1910 Playing tennis outside the homestead, Nive Downs – Courtesy State Library of Queensland

Meeting the mail coach – Courtesy State Library of Queensland

Chapter Nine

From coaching to motor buggies

COBB AND CO.
By Will H. Ogilvie

The bullock driver scarcely feels
His way on new-cut track,
Ere Cobb & Co., with lighter wheels,
Have run the marks outback;
And while the seasons come and go,
And through the changing years,
All flags are dipped to Cobb & Co.,
The Western pioneers;
What reck, if all the creeks be dry?
And hot winds blight and glow,
We'll meet and fill our glasses high,
Good luck to Cobb & Co.

(Cobb and Co., Verse 4, 20 Apr 1895, p.9)

The last coach

"Slowly but surely of late years the horse coach has been disappearing from many parts, of the State Queensland, until earlier in the week there appeared in our columns, that on August 14, the last horse-coach trip of the world-renowned firm of Cobb and Co. had been run from Surat to Yeulba. Cobb and Co. have played a leading part in the development of out-back Queensland and the announcement above referred to has been received with not a little sentimental regret by the many thousands who have during the long career of the Surat-Yeulba coach ... travelled by it. The motor coach has come in its place, but memory of the old conditions will long survive ... The coach, with its leather springs arid six to eight horses, gave in many cases a much more comfortable ride than upon some of the branch railway lines on the Darling Downs, and the worst portion of the journey was that over the corduroy ... It may be mentioned that in the heyday of their service Cobb and Co. had about 50 mail coaches running in Queensland, with a stable of 1,500 horses." (The Last Coach, 29 Aug 1924, p.10)

The motor buggy arrived

By 1909, the arrival of the motor buggy was beginning to transform inland transportation. One report noted: "Mr J. W. B. Waterhouse last week drove out to St. Clair, to Mr Onslow's place, in a motor buggy. The route is over some of the worst roads in the country, but the 18 miles were covered in an hour and a half, and the return journey was accomplished in 20 minutes less time. Mr Waterhouse is convinced that the motor buggies will prove a most popular method of locomotion for country roads, as the vehicle which he tested ran very smoothly." (Motor Buggies, 20 Jul 1909, p.2)

The following year, enthusiasm for motor transport was growing. "Mr. Lawrence writes:—I should much regret to have to return to the horse-drawn vehicle, and to do away with more horses. I have another motor waggon to arrive during next week. My first waggon is a 6-h.p. two-cylinder, air-cooled engine ... A PLEA FOR THE MOTOR BUGGY.—The motor buggy is slowly but surely making headway in Australia. When first introduced it was the object, naturally, of great curiosity amongst the general public and the motorist ... There are several types of motor buggies in Australia and in almost every instance they have proved the highest efficiency and reliability on the roughest of country roads." (Motor Notes, 28 Apr 1910, p.35)

By 1915, motoring had become a feature of everyday public life. In Surat: "Mr. Godfrey Morgan, M.L.A., arrived by motor car on Thursday, and addressed the electors in the Shire Council's Hall the same evening ... stirring and impressive speech ... During his term he had been responsible for the building of no less than forty schools in the Murilla electorate ... He was also the means of the Tara railway line being pushed on towards Surat, and he expected this line to reach us within a couple of years. He was going to fight hard for that project ... Mr. Morgan left for the Coomrith district by buggy on Friday morning in the rain ... The weather to-night looks frosty." (Surat, 19 May 1915, p.3)

SYMBOLIC SHIFT

By 1921, the transition from horse to motor transport was visibly underway. The symbolic shift was marked in Charleville: "VALE COBB & CO. The passing of the old and the coming of the new was exemplified in our town last week (says the Charleville correspondent of the N.Q. Register), when Herriman Bros., motor mechanics and general engineers, took possession of Cobb & Co.'s factory, which they purchased recently from that company." (Vale Cobb and Co., 16 Jun 1921, p.6)

Two years later, Cobb and Co.'s legendary coach empire *had been reduced to a single route.*

"For the year to June 30 Cobb and Co., Ltd, reports a net profit £3011, after providing for depreciation ... The once great pioneering organisation of the eastern portion of Australia has now only one line of coaches, that from Yeulba to Thallon ... Coach-works and coaches have disappeared with the advent of the motor-car, and to-day the firm's principal activities centre in supplying all requirements to pastoralists and others in the bush." (Cobb and Co., 20 Oct 1923, p.4)

EXIT COBB'S

By September 1924, the last coach operating under the Cobb and Co. name, running between Yeulba and Surat, was to be withdrawn and replaced by a motor car."The last coach, under the famous name of Cobb and Co., plying between Yeulba and Surat, Queensland, will be withdrawn this month, and its place will be taken by a motor car ...

Who is there among the older generation of Australians, who can hear, without regret, and a sense of what we all owe to them, of the last of Cobb's coaches, to disappear forever from the back country roads of the Commonwealth? Some of us knew them when they, under several firm names, were the only passenger and mail vehicles that traded regularly between many of the towns of the country, and the railway centres. Most of us have been passengers by these coaches. We travelled with strange company, and often in discomfort, but safely, and in ordinary weather, to a reasonable time-table.

What men the drivers of Cobb's old coaches were— good, all-round men, plucky, resourceful, obliging, and the friends of all conditions of folk along their route.

What memories we have of the country youngsters, boy or girl, or the older folk in a cart, waiting for the coach, not so much for the mail, though the Sydney weekly papers years ago used to be a great joy, but for, the storekeeper's parcel of clothing and groceries and so forth from the nearest town.

With these, his friends, the driver would exchange the news of the district, and when the little conference broke up, and the residents took leave of the coach, how often they stayed to watch the only link they knew with the big world, as it disappeared for a week.

Great names are associated with Cobb and Co.'s services, such as those of the late James Rutherford, of Bathurst, and the late Walter Hall, of Sydney.

Though it is years now since the railways; and then the motor cars, displaced many of the old coaches, there was, up to recently, a wide net-work of these services spread all over out-back Australia. A fine service it was, full of peculiar Australian characteristics, casual, happy-go-lucky in many ways, marked by good fellowship, good humor, courage, and an immense patience with the weather, the vicissitudes of the road, and the extraordinary development of out-of-the-way human traits." (Exit Cobb's, 5 Sep 1924, p.3)

Coach preservation

At the time the last coach ran, Alderman William Brooks called for the preservation of the final coach. "The last coach controlled by Cobb and Co. is running between Yeulba and Surat, Queensland…

Ald. William Brooks. M.L.C., president of the Australian Federal Capital League, suggests that the coach be permanently housed in the National Museum at Canberra." (Cobb's Coach at Canberra, 24 Aug 1924, p.6)

However, the Commonwealth Government "declined to adopt the suggestion that the last of Cobb and Co.'s coaches should be preserved in the National Museum at Canberra. Senator Pearce has informed Ald. William Brooks, M.L.C., president of the Australian Federal Capital League, that consideration has been given to the practicability of preserving for posterity the last coach run by Cobb and Co.

The Federal Government, it is added, recognised the prominent part played by Cobb's coaches in the early history of the nation. It is pointed out, however, that it will be some considerable time before steps can be taken to establish a national museum, and that there is at present no suitable accommodation at Canberra for the housing and custody of the coach. In the circumstances the Minister regrets that he is unable to act upon the suggestion made by the league. The chairman has urged the Minister to reconsider his decision. He points out that it should not be difficult to find some outhouse or stable or some sort of cover at Canberra where the coach would be protected from the weather and from vandalism, until a permanent home could be found.

And Brooks is now seeking the sympathetic support in this matter of Mr. Theodore, Premier of Queensland, in whose State the last coach is now ending its career of usefulness, prior to being deposed by a motor car which will be used for coach purposes." (Last Coach. Its Preservation. Federal Attitude., 4 Sep 1924, p.8)

"Cobb's coach will be on the showgrounds for the last time this year. It was the last Cobb coach to carry the Royal Mail in Queensland—perhaps even in all of Australia—and it may interest thousands of people. This coach has been purchased by the Federal Government and will, it is believed, be sent to a museum in the south. Why should it be removed from Queensland? I feel that it is Queensland's right to have this historic relic of the early pioneering days in our state, preserved forever within the Queensland Museum. —Mr Ernest Baynes, President of the Royal National Association" (Not for Queensland, 3 Aug 1926, p.14)

In 1939, the question remained: where was the last coach? "You state that the last Cobb and Co. coach was taken off the Yeulba-Surat (Q.) run, and that this coach is now in the Queensland Museum. This is not so. I think Mr. J. H. M. Abbott made the same mistake in an article in 'The World's News' some years ago. At the time, knowing that the statement was incorrect, I got in touch with Mr. Heber A. Longman, Director of the Queensland Museum, who advised me (January 5, 1933), as follows:—*I have to inform you that we have no Cobb and Co.'s coach in the Queensland Museum. The Cobb's coach that was in Brisbane is now at Canberra. This coach was used in the Travel and Transport Pageant organised by the Royal National Association during Show Week, 1925. Lord Forster rode in the coach on that occasion. Owing to its size, the Cobb's coach was never on exhibition in the Queensland Museum …*

Several bodies of Cobb's coaches are yet to be seen at Charleville (Q), where they are used for playhouses for children. Incidentally, the spelling of Yeulba has during the past few months been altered to 'Yuleba' (which should have been the spelling in the first place, but a careless railway employee, in putting up the name at the station, arranged the metal letters to read 'Yeulba,' and thus it remained for more than 40 years. However, this has now been altered, and the P.O. has also adopted the spelling 'Yuleba.' Perhaps you have heard the story of how the place got its name. In the very early days an Irishman settled there and went in for sheep. He also had a few goats to supply him with milk. One day while he was milking, a rather wild 'nanny,' a surveyor rode up and asked the selector the name of the place. With the bellowing of the goat the Irishman did not hear the stranger speak, neither did he observe his approach, and sinking his boot into the ribs of the goat, he said. 'You'll bah, you—!' And Yeulba it remained. Thank you very much, F.B.A., for your letter. Our information was obtained from the 'Australian Encyclopaedia,' which is usually correct with its facts. We feel that your letter will interest a wide section of our readers." (Cobb and Co., 29 Jul 1939, p.45)

A final reflection, noted in 1924, was as much about the future as it was about the past: "Mr. Theodore, Premier of Queensland …

> the last coach is now ending its career of usefulness … a motor car … will be used for coach purposes."

(Last Coach, 4 Sep 1924, p.8)

1890 Last coach leaving Warrnambool – Courtesy Corangamite Regional Library, Picture Victoria

1924 Last Cobb and Co.'s Coach, being used between Yeulba and Surat – Courtesy National Library of Australia

ca. 1922 Girls' hostel in Wells Street, Charleville – Courtesy State Library of Queensland

Dalby Railway Station – Courtesy State Library of Queensland

View of a street in Drayton (Sir J. R. Kemp) – Courtesy State Library of Queensland

Car travelling on a road in Greenmount (Sir J. R. Kemp) – Courtesy State Library of Queensland

Warwick Road, Toowoomba (Sir J. R. Kemp) – Courtesy State Library of Queensland

Car parked next to closed gate near Barcaldine (Sir J. R. Kemp) – Courtesy State Library of Queensland

An extra snippet ...

COBB & CO.'S COACHES STOPS:

BRISBANE "Brisbane to Ipswich, Toowoomba, Warwick, Dalby, Condamine, Roma ... leave Royal Hotel, Queen-street ... H. T. Millie, General Manager ... Brisbane to Sandgate ... H. Wakefield, Proprietor." (Classified Advertising, 4 Jan 1868, p.1) "Brisbane, Ipswich, and Toowoomba ... leave Younge's Royal Hotel, North Brisbane and Nolan's Royal Mail Hotel, South Brisbane." (Classified Advertising, 21 Feb 1866, p.1) "Mr. Hanran ... having for many years kept the North Star Hotel, on the site of Mr. John M'Grath's present commodious buildings, at the corner of Brisbane and Ellenborough Streets ... During the sixties the North Star was the headquarters of the coaches of the widely known firm of Cobb and Co." (Local and General News, 24 Dec 1895, p.4)

IPSWICH "Brisbane, Ipswich, and Toowoomba ... leave Hanran's North Star Hotel, Ipswich." (Fifty Years Ago, 25 Mar 1916, p.12)

TOOWOOMBA "Toowoomba to Brisbane ... leaving Fraser's Hotel, Toowoomba ... Martin Haughton, agent." (Advertising, 6 Mar 1866, p.4) "Mr. Fraser's Hotel, in Ruthven-street." (Toowoomba Police Court, 15 Aug 1866, p.2) "Captain Witham kept the Queen's Arms, at the corner of Ruthven and Margaret streets, from which place Cobb and Co 's coaches started for Brisbane." (Memories of a Pioneer, 21 Jun 1924, p.18)

WARWICK "Toowoomba to Warwick ... leaves Fleming's, Downs Hotel, Warwick and Mr. Fraser's Queen's Arms Hotel, Toowoomba." (Advertising, 6 Mar 1866, p.4) "Commercial Hotel corner of Palmerin and Victoria Streets, Warwick ... Booking Office for Cobb and Co.'s Royal Telegraph Line of Mai Coaches." (Advertising, 14 Feb 1867, p.4)

DALBY "Cobb & Co.'s ... leave Gibson's Caledonian Hotel, Dalby." (Advertising, 4 Oct 1866, p.1) "Criterion Hotel, Dalby. T. Howe, Proprietor. Booking Office for Cobb and Co.'s coaches." (Advertising, 1 Apr 1871, p.1)

COBB & CO.'S STABLES LOCATIONS:

BRISBANE "Fire ... Albert-street ... destroyed the stables occupied by Messrs. Cobb and Co." (Telegraphic, 22 Aug 1871, p.2) "The first stables were in Albert-street, Brisbane, on the site now occupied by Messrs. Fleming & Sons ironmongers ... new premises were obtained where the Queensland Machinery Co.'s premises now stand, and later on at the junction of Queen-street and Petrie Bight, where is now Joliffe's showroom and near Uhl's saddlery works. Both of these were old employees of Cobb's and shareholders." (The Genesis of Cobb & Co., 15 Sep 1917, p.11)

IPSWICH "O'Sullivan's Family Hotel ... in East-street (latterly known as the residence of Mr. Geo. Wilson) ... A portion of the property also was utilised by Messrs. Cobb & Co., for stabling their horses and quarters, after Cobb & Co. had put on their line of mail coaches to run between Ipswich and Brisbane, and vice-versa." (Glimpses of Ipswich History, 24 Oct 1923, p.9)

TOOWOOMBA "Fire broke out in a range of stables belonging to Mr. Fraser, of the Queen's Arms Hotel ... The stables were used by Messrs. Cobb and Co." (Toowoomba, 20 Mar 1867, p.3)

MILES "The Sportsman's Arms Hotel, Billiard Room, Saddler's Shop, Cobb and Co.'s Stables—the whole forming one of the largest and most commodious Hotels on the Western Road." (Advertising, 24 Dec 1878, p.4)

ROMA "Messrs. Cobb and Co.'s stables, at Moore's Hotel, Roma, have been burned to the ground." (Brisbane, 6 Jun 1878, p.4)

THE DAYS OF COBB & CO.
By G. M. Smith

We have Telephones and Cables And Electric Telegraph,
To flash the news to any point In a minute and a half.
To sum it up what way you will, It's anything but slow ;
It seems a vast improvement On the days of Cobb & Co.

We have electric trams and Cable trams, The Motor and the Bike ;
You can get about the country now At any speed you like.
We have railways to the back blocks, Where the iron horses go,
And yet the times were better In the days of Cobb & Co.

There was enterprise and money And any amount of work ;
There was wool and fat stock rolling in From the Mitchell plains round Bourke.
There was merchandise and passengers To carry to and fro ;
There was life too, in Australia, In the days of Cobb & Co.

To travel out a thousand miles You'd book yourself in town ;
They'd guarantee to pull you through, When you paid your money down.
They travelled then by rough bush tracks, Through mountains, bog and snow,
And deliver you well up to time, Would good old Cobb & Co.

And they had some splendid drivers, Who could handle horses neat ;
To see them work their ribbons on Those bush tracks was a treat.
And they'd get a change of coaches Every twenty miles or so ;
And they drove some slashing cattle In the days of Cobb & Co.

Our progress has been rapid, But the days are poorer now,
Than the days of Jimmy Tyson, and Good old Jackey Dow.
I remember well the sixties, And transit then was slow ;
But give to me the golden days, The days of Cobb & Co.

(The Days of Cobb & Co., 4 Mar 1904 , p.4)

1881 Cobb's Coach leaving Bourke Street –
Illustrated Australian News, 29 Jan 1881, p.1

Appendices

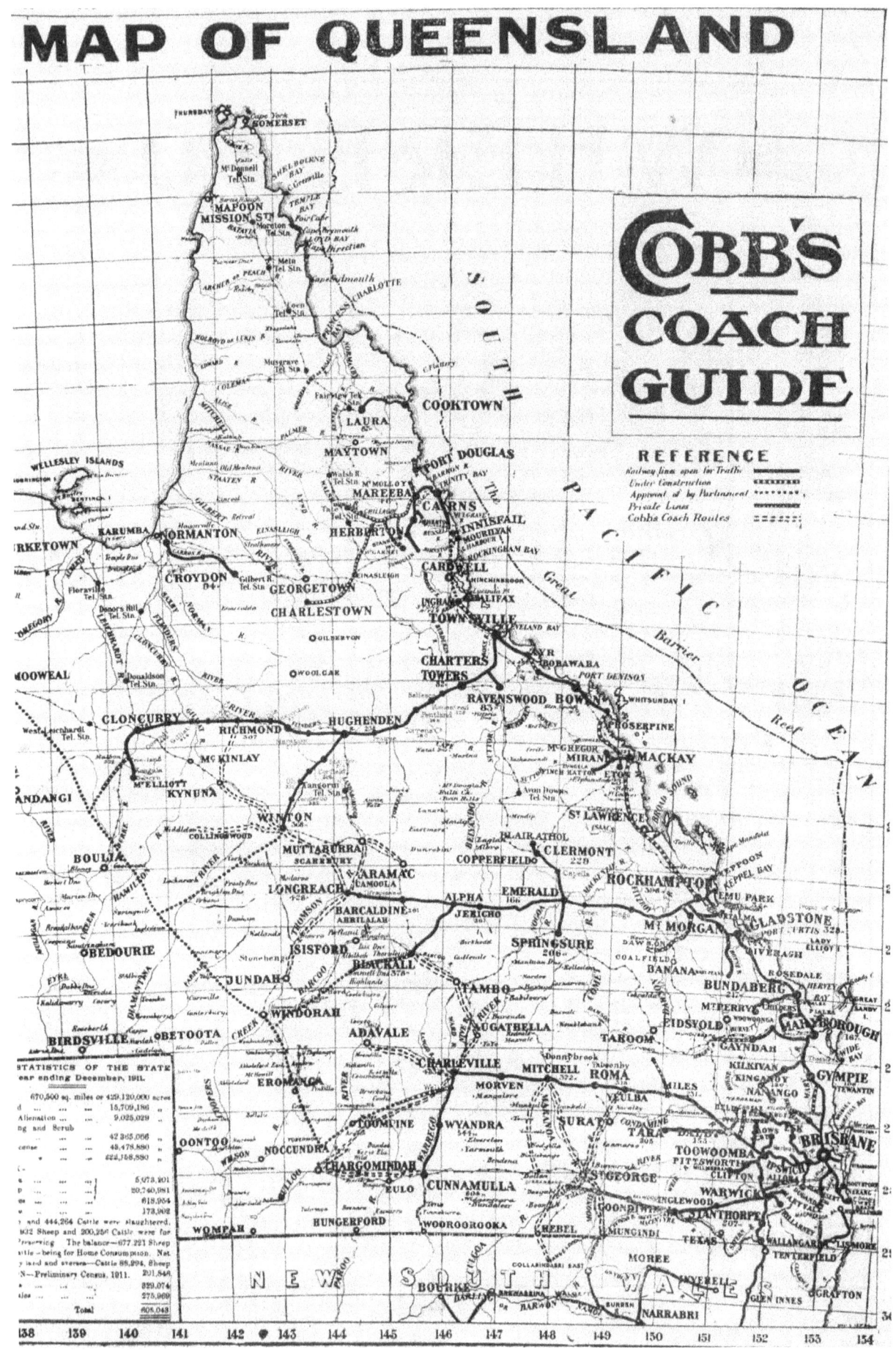

1.1 Map of Queensland, Cobb's Coach Routes – Coaching in Australia, a history of the coaching firm Cobb and Co., W. Lees, p.3

THE AUSTRALIAN CONVEYANCE,
OR
NEW ROYAL MAIL COACH.

WILL Start from the DUKE OF WELLINGTON, Parramatta, every Morning at 7 o'clock.
Fare—Inside, 5s. Outside, 3s.

Cobb and Co's.,
TELEGRAPH LINE OF COACHES, TO THE LACHLAN.

ON and after THURSDAY the 4th July a Six Horse Coach will leave COBB & CO's Booking Office, Bathurst, Every

Thursday, Saturday & Tuesday

For the Lachlan via Orange,

Arriving at Lachlan same Evenings and returning from there Every MONDAY, WEDNESDAY and FRIDAYS.

For particulars apply at COBB and CO'S Office, Bathurst.

JAMES RUTHERFORD,
Manager N.S.W.

TO LET.

A PUBLIC HOUSE, in first-rate trade, known as the "Red Cow," admirably situated in the principal street of Ipswich, and doing a first-rate business, the present tenant retiring in consequence of ill-health. Stock-in-Trade and Furniture to be taken at a valuation. Early application necessary, so as to insure the certificate of license in April next, and possession of the premises to be given on the 1st July instant.

For further particulars apply to the proprietor Mr. WILLIAM HORTON, Bull's Head Inn, Drayton; or to,

A. E. CAMPBELL,
Auctioneer and Commission Agent.
Ipswich, Feb. 23.

2.1 1827 Advertising – The Monitor, 30 Aug 1827, p.2
2.2 1862 Advertising – Bathurst Free Press and Mining Journal, 28 Jun 1862, p.3
2.3 1852 Classified Advertising, Mr. William Horton, Bull's Head Inn, Drayton – The Moreton Courier, 20 Mar 1852, p.1
2.4 Mr. Lawrence's costs after 12 months (Cost of a car compared to horses) – Punch, 28 Apr 1910, p.35

COST OF CAR.			
Cost of petrol	£41	0	0
Tyres and sundries	£40	0	0
Miles run, 12,000.			
COST OF HORSES.			
Cost of four horses, say	£124	0	0
Repairs to harness	£37	0	0
Miles run, say 8000.			

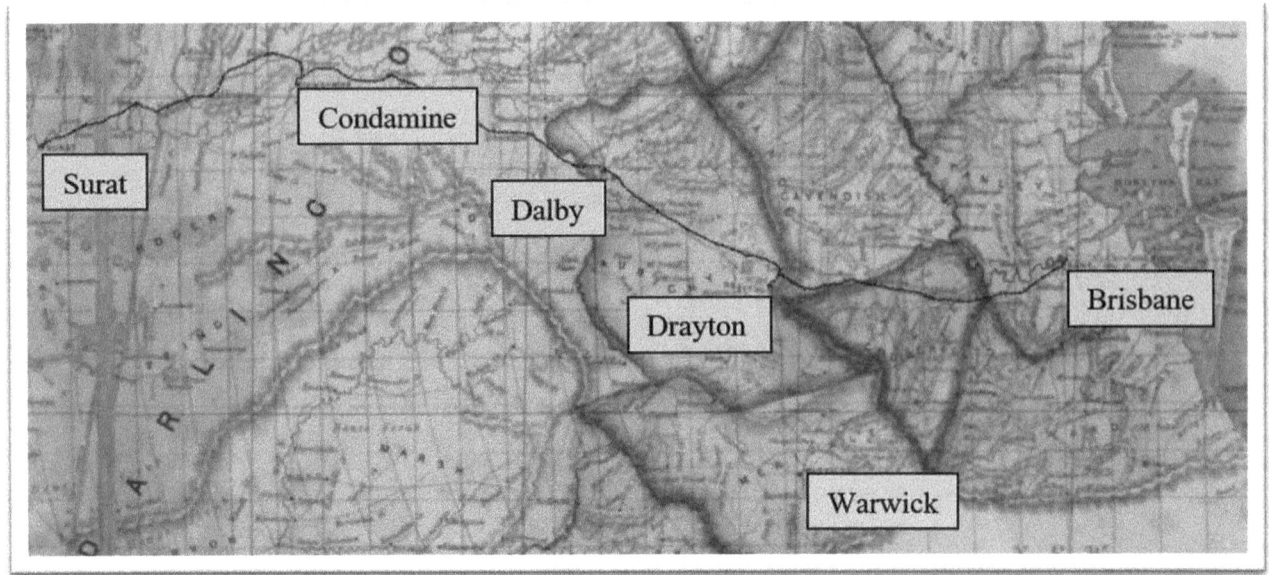

2.5 1863 Map of Queensland, showing road between Drayton, Dalby, Condamine and Surat
– Courtesy National Library of Australia

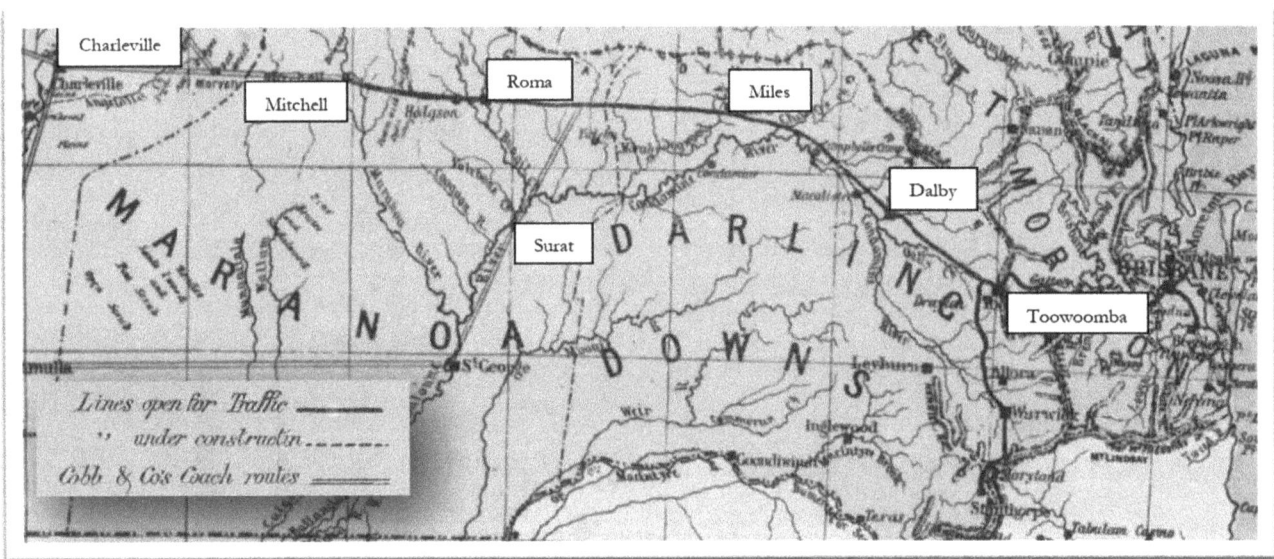

2.6 1885 Map of Queensland (Cobb and Co's Coach Routes)
– Courtesy National Library of Australia

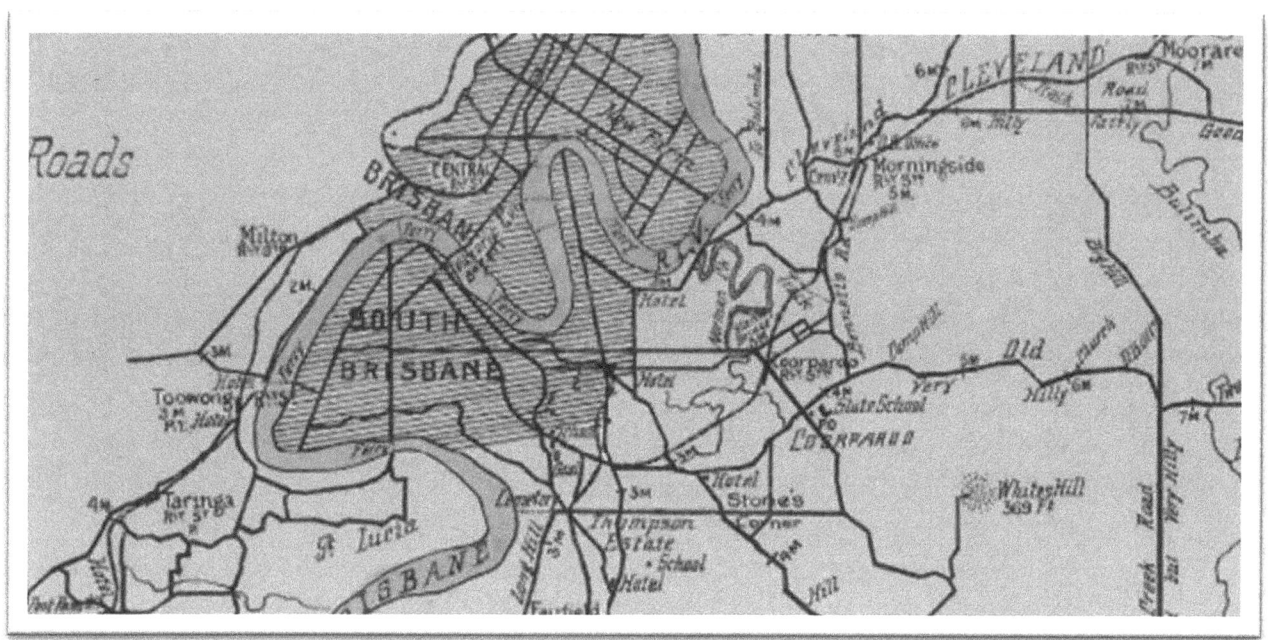

2.7 1840 Brisbane Town – Courtesy The University of Queensland

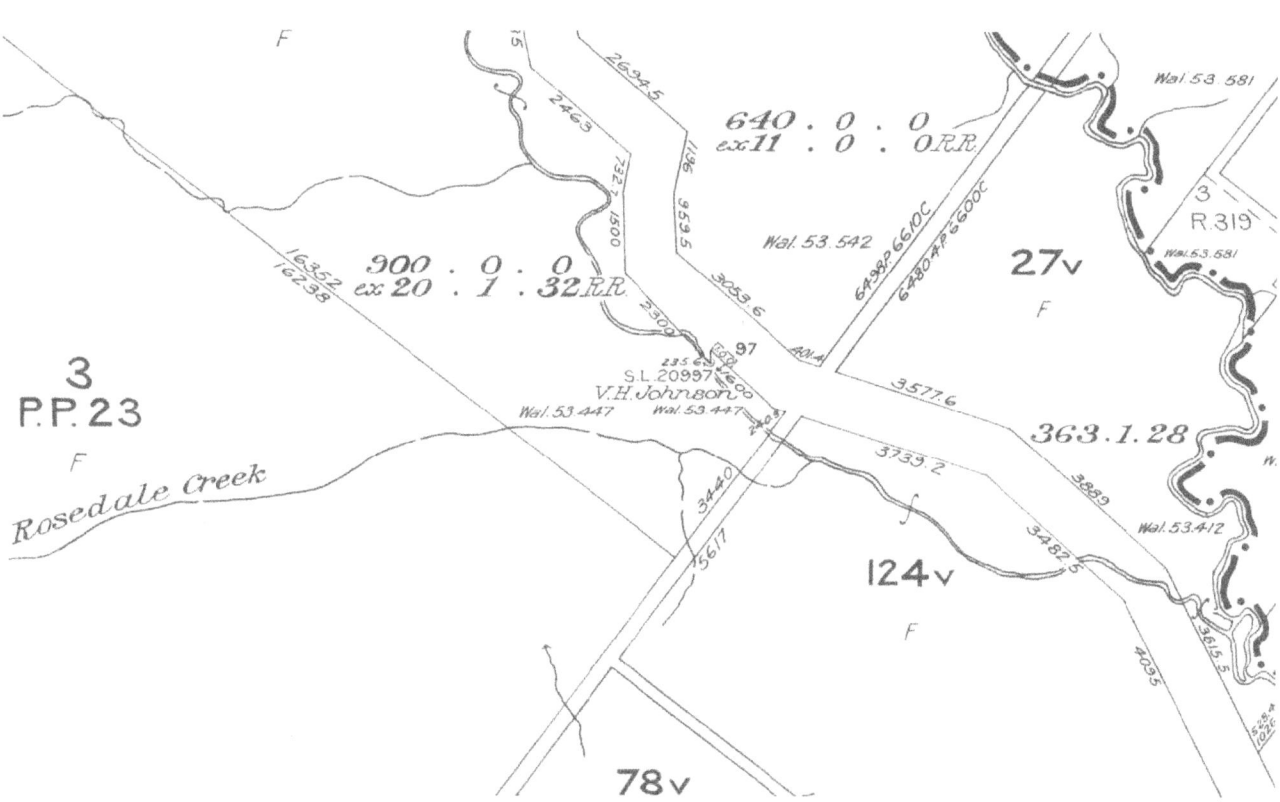

2.8 Old slab hut original site – Parish of Hodgson, County of Waldegrave, Map

3.1 Conveyance of mails

1. From and to Brisbane and Ipswich daily.
2. Ditto Brisbane and Ipswich by express Mails when required.
3. Ditto Brisbane and Cleveland, once a week.
4. Ditto Toowoomba, Drayton, and Dalby, twice a week.
5. Ditto Toowoomba, Drayton, and Gundiwindi via Canal Creek, once a week.
6. Ditto Toowoomba, Drayton, Warwick, and Maryland, once a week.
7. Ditto Dalby and Condamine via Daandine, Warra, and Wombo, once a week.
8. Ditto Dalby and Goondiwindi via St Ruth's, Cecil's Plains, Dunmore, Western Creek, and Retreat, once a week.
9. Ditto Warwick and Ipswich via Cunningham's Gap, twice a week.
10. Ditto Warwick and Leyburn, once a week.
11. Ditto Gayndah and Maryborough, once a week.
12. Ditto Gayndah and Taroom via Dykehead, Yeccilla, and Hawkwood, once a week.
13. Ditto Taroom and Rockhampton, once a fortnight.
14. Ditto Westwood and Nulalbin, once a fortnight.
15. Ditto Maryborough and Gladstone, once a week.
16. Ditto Rockhampton and Marlborough, once a week.

4.1 Tenders for mail service

- Toowoomba and Dalby, via Jondaryan, Cobb and Co., Brisbane, £665, one year, three times a week, four-horse coach.
- Toowoomba and Drayton, Rodger Mara, Toowoomba, £65, twice a day, horse.
- Toowoomba and Warwick, via Allora and Spring Creek, Cobb and Co., Brisbane, £721, one year, three times a week, four-horse coach.
- Toowoomba and Goondiwindi, via Drayton, Leyburn, and Inglewood, Henry Byrnes, Leyburn, £270, two years, once a week, horse.
- Toowoomba and Railway Station, Fred Wockener, Toowoomba, £65, two years, twice a day, except Sunday, coach.

5.1 Country Directory—Mail routes 1864
(Pugh's Queensland almanac and directory and law calendar, 1864, pp.190-193)

- IPSWICH AND DRAYTON MAIL "Remarks.—The mail contractor makes the distance to Laidley 28 miles, thence to Gatton 12 miles, and thence to Toowoomba 25. At Alfred, 18 miles from Ipswich, a small township has been formed. The Red Lion Inn, Moore's, is 7 miles on the road, and the Rising Sim at Rosewood is 14 miles on. The head station of Franklin Vale, Messrs. Mort and Laidley's, is about 12 miles from Laidley, on Bremer Waters. Laidley is a small but beautifully situated township, surrounded by rich open land on the banks of the creek. There are four inns there, and other trading establishments. On Sandy Creek, about three miles from Laidley, there are several farms, situated on excellent land, lightly timbered. At Gatton a first-rate bridge now spans the creek. Rosewood station is eight miles from Laidley, on the Lockyer, and about the same distance from Gatton; Tarampa is about 16 miles from either place; Buaraba, Mr. J. P. Bell's, is about 17 miles from Laidley; and Franklin Vale is about 12 miles from Laidley, and about 25 miles from Ipswich."

- IPSWICH AND WARWICK "Remarks.—Adjacent to this line is Normandy Plains Station, Mr. G. Thorn's, 20 miles from Ipswich; Rosevale, Mr. Patrick Mayne's, 27 miles from Ipswich; Maroon, Mr. J. Carden Collins', at Mount Walker, on the heads of the Logan; Coochin Coochin, also Mr. Collins', at Dalhunty Plains, on the head of Teviot Brook; Dugandan, Mrs. M'Donald's, six miles from Coochin, down the Teviot; and Undullah, late Mr. J. Cameron's, also on the Teviot."

- TOOWOOMBA, WARWICK, AND MARYLAND MAIL "Remarks.—Warwick is the nearest town to the southern frontier of Queensland. In the neighborhood there are several large stations, namely—Canning Downs, Mr. G. Davidson's, 2 miles from Warwick; Rosenthal, Aberdeen Company, 2 miles; South Toolburra, Aberdeen Company, 14 miles; North Toolburra, Mr. Donald Gunn's, 7 miles; Gladfield, part of Maryvale, 12 miles; Killarney, Mr. G. Davidson's, 17 miles; Talgai, Messrs. Clark and Hanmer's, 25 miles; Pikedale, Donald Gunn's, 50 miles; Pike's Creek, R. H. Bloomfield's, 55 miles; Ballandean, H. H. Nicol's, 55 miles; Nundubbermere, J. M. Thompson's, 45 miles; Mongola, 65 miles; Maidenhead, 90 miles; and Undercliff, Mr. M. Spearing's, 50 miles. Goomburra, Messrs. Hodgson, M'Lean, and Green's, is 15 miles from Warwick. Besides Mr. Marsh's station at Maryland, there are two other stations in New South Wales supplied from the Warwick post-office, namely—Acacia Creek, Reid and Marsh's, 22 miles, and Koreelah, 30 miles. Warwick is the finest wheat growing locality in all Queensland, and a fine flour-mill has been erected there by Mr. C. Clark. Allora is a small township situated on Dalrymple Creek, about 12 miles from Pilton Station, and containing about 150 inhabitants. The land is lightly timbered, and excellently adapted for agriculture. There are about 50 farms under cultivation. A gold-field has recently been proclaimed at Talgai, where several diggers are now at work. It consists principally of rich quartz reefs."

- TOOWOOMBA, DRAYTON, AND GOONDIWINDI MAIL "Remarks.—Glenelg, Mr. J. M'Arthur's, is about 20 miles south of Gillespie's; Warroo, Mr. F. Bracker's, is 70 miles from Warwick, but off this line; and Beebo, late R. Young's, and Texas, Mr. M'Dougall's, are supplied by this route. There are two routes from Warwick to Warroo, both equal in distance, viz.—either by way of Pikedale, or by way of Canal Creek and Glenelg."

- TOOWOOMBA, DRAYTON, AND DALBY MAIL "Remarks.—The site of a village, to be called Bowenville, has been surveyed close to Phipps's station, at the Long Water Hole. The lines to Condamine, Goondiwindi, and Auburn branch off at Dalby. The town is situated on Myall about 5 miles from the Condamine River, and lies low and flat. The station of Cumkillinbar, Mr. T. De Lacy Moffatt's, late Balfour's, on Myall Creek, is in the neighborhood. Dalby is 138 miles from Brisbane, the route being—Brisbane to Ipswich, 24 miles. Ipswich to Toowoomba, 61 miles; and Toowoomba to Dalby, 53 mls. Rosalie Plains, the station of Messrs. Kent and Wienholt, is about 28 miles west of Dalby. The distance from the Inn at Jondaryan to Dalby is 26 miles."

- DALBY AND CONDAMINE MAIL "Remarks.—The above is the present mail route, a spring-cart being used as a conveyance, and the crossing of the Condamine at two points being avoided. Formerly the route was as follows:—Dalby to Greenbank, 5 miles; thence to Daandine, 15 miles; thence to Warra (G. Thorn's), 12 miles; thence to Campbell's Camp (Wallace's), 8 miles; thence to Chinchilla (Gibson and Buchanan's), 17 miles; and from thence to Condamine, via Wombo, 41 miles. At Kogan Creek (on the present mail line), there is a village, the distance from which to the surrounding stations is as follows: To Wombo, 26 miles; to Chinchilla, 16 miles; to Warra Warra head station, 12 miles; to overseer's station, 17 miles; to Daandine, 15 miles. The lines to Surat, Roma, and Taroom branch off from Condamine, which is a rising township, where a Court of Petty Sessions is held. At Greenbank a bridge is erected across the Condamine. At Campbell's Camp there is an inn, formerly kept by Mr. Wallace, the mail contractor; and at a short distance from the head station of Wombo there is a house of accommodation."

- CONDAMINE AND ROMA MAIL "Remarks.—The post-office will be removed to Roma from Bungeworgorai (5 miles distant) early this year. Roma is a thriving young township on Bungill Creek, and is likely to become a place of some importance. Although formed but recently, there were, in June last (1863), three stores and two inns there. It is situated on the present main line of road to the Warrego, and it is anticipated that a postal line will shortly be established between Roma, by way of the Maranoa, towards the Second Crossing Place, where a township will probably be proclaimed, and where there are now two inns. Bungeworgorai was formerly known as Mount Abundance. In the vicinity of this route there are several stations, viz. :—Bin Bin, Mr. F. A. Forbes', 8 miles from Condamine ; Alderton, Messrs. H. Coxen and Co., 20 miles from ditto; Wan-dai Gumbal, old police station on Tchanning Creek ; Moongool, Mr. Marks', 15 miles from Bendemere southerly; Dingham and Yuelba, Messrs. Tom, 14 miles from Moongool, ditto ; Warkon, Mr. Barlow's, 9 miles from Dingham, ditto. Combabala is north of Bendemere. South of Bungill Downs and Bungeworgorai there are near at hand, Mr. Wilkie's station on Bungill Creek; Mr. Spencer's, at Deepwater ; and Mr. Coxen's, on Yalebone Creek. Going west of Bungewor-gorai, there is Bindango, Messrs. Kennedy and Rae's, 10 miles distant; thence to Sim's, on the Ambi, 22 miles ; thence to Mr. Morey's, on the Maranoa, 17 miles; thence to Native Police Barracks, 26 miles ; thence Forest Vale, 20 miles ; thence to Messrs. Moffatt and Fullerton's, 10 miles ; and thence to Womblebank, Messrs. Ferrett and Warnod's, 10 miles."

- ROMA AND MARANOA. NEW LINE. As stated in the foregoing, it is probable that a mail line will be established early in this year between Roma and the crossing place on the Maranoa, the route of which will be as follows:– Roma to Bungeworgorai, Old Bindango, Deedes and Fos-ter's, Police Barracks, crossing-place on Maranoa = 86 miles. This route may be altered after the mailman has commenced running, should he strike a more convenient line. The stations &c., on, or in the vicinity of, this line are as follows Mitchell Downs, Messrs. Morey and Co.'s ; Wa-roonga, Messrs. Deedes and Foster's ; Forest Vale, Tooth and Co.'s ; Eurella, Hunter and Fosberry's; Mongallala (beyond Mitchell Downs), Turn-bull and Co.; Angellala, Maclean and Co.'s ; T. S. Sadleir's, Harrison and Co.'s, and Cameron and Co.'s stations; Merivale (beyond Forest Vale), J. Ferrett's ; Appletree Creek, Moffatt and Fullerton's; Merivale (2), —, Smyth's; Yeo, J. Norman; Kennedy and Rae's; Ward River, Wiseman's; Bai-ley and M'Andrew's, Bullmore and Co.'s, and Thom Brothers, on the Warrego ; Agenthulla, Ashmore's ; and Nive ; S. Spencer's. The present head station of Bindango is about 4 miles, S. by W., of Old Bindango, which is now an overseer's station. Morey's is 22 miles from the junction of the Ambi with the Maranoa ; the Native Police Barracks are 30 miles above him; and the place where the new township will probably be formed (Fleming's Crossing) is 12 miles above the barracks. Deedes and Foster's is 12 miles from Morey's, and Deuchar and Lee's is 15 miles due north of it. Symes' is on the road to Morey's, 18 miles from Deedes and Foster's, and 27 from Bindango. Merivale Creek, on the lower part of which Fer-rett's is situated, is 12 miles from Forest Vale. Smyth's is on a creek between Box Creek and the Merivale ; 25 miles above him, towards Mount Hutton Range is Vernon's, on Box Creek, 15 miles from Merivale, and 12 miles from Moffatt and Fullerton's, who are on Appletree Creek, 10 miles from Forest Vale, back of Kennedy and Rae's. Forest Vale is 4 miles above Fleming's Crossing. Possession Creek runs into the Maranoa River 20 miles above Forest Vale, and M'Andrew's is located 10 miles up that creek, and 22 miles from Forest Vale."

6.1 Mail services

- THALLON, ON THE SOUTH-WESTERN LINE, SOUTH TO MUNGINDI ON THE BARWON RIVER, NSW BORDER   33 miles
- THALLON, NORTH TO ST. GEORGE, SURAT, AND YEULBA, ON THE WESTERN LINE   182 miles
- ST. GEORGE TO MITCHELL   152 miles
- MITCHELL TO BOLLON   148 miles
- CUNNAMULLA TO THARGOMINDAH   135 miles
- CHARLEVILLE TO TAMBO   134 miles
- LONGREACH TO JUNDAH   154 miles
- LONGREACH TO WINTON   128 miles

7.1 1901 Postal Directory—examples
(Pugh's Queensland almanac and directory, 1901)

- CHARLEVILLE AND COONGOOLA MAIL STAGE. Mail Route. Charleville to Riversleigh, 40 miles; Boatman, 45; Yarmouth, via Elmira and Elverston, 58; Coongoola Mail Stage, 23. Total, 166 miles.

- CHARLEVILLE AND ADAVALE. Mail Route. Charley ille to Glengarry, 7 miles; thence to Buriandilla, 27; Langlo, 39; Adavale, 43. Total, 116 miles.

- CHARLEVILLE AND ADAVALE. Mail Route.

- CHARLEVILLE AND AUTHORINGA. Riversleigh, 26; thence to Authoringa, 14. Total, 40 miles.

- CHARLEVILLE TO EULO. Charleville to Gowrie, 12 miles; thence to Bowen, 21; Yarrovale, 30; Bierbank, 19; Bechal, 30; Mt. Alfred, 20; Humeburn, 20; Tilboroo, 35; Eulo, 25. Total, 212 miles.

- CHARLEVILLE AND BLACK ALL. Mail Route. Charleville to Gowrie, 14 miles; thence to Nive Junction, 17; Augathella, 21; Nive Downs, 25; Tambo, 51; Greendale, 7; Ennis killen, 21; Northampton, 20; Blackall, 27. Total, 203 miles.

- CHARLEVILLE AND MINNIE DOWNS. Charleville to Millie (Gordon and Flood), 20 miles; thence to Burrandilla (Martin and Co), 21; Khamooinulga, 20; Mount Morris, 25; Langlo Downs, 27; Minnie Downs, 32. Total, 145 miles. Ambathella Station, Williams' and Mentone Station, are served by this line.

- CHARLEVILLE AND MOONGARRTE. Charleville to Burbank, 82 miles; thence to Bechal, 30; Mount Alfred, 20; Humeburn, 20. Tilboroo, 35; Moongarrie 25. Total, 212 miles.

- CHARLEVILLE AND TAMBO. Mail Route. Charleville to Gowrie Cattle Station, 30 miles, thence, to Nive Junction, 4 miles; Augathella, 22; Biddenham, 12; Oakwood. 25; Landowne, 22; Mitoura, 32; Tambo, 12. Total, 159 miles.

- DALBY AND GOONDIWINDI. Mail Route. Dalby to St. Ruth's, 15 miles; thence to Tipton, 2; Cecil Plains, 8; Kurrawah, 10; Condamine Plains, 4; Turallin, 12; Western Creek, 9; Woondool, 30; Wyaga, 20; Yagaburne, 10; back to Wyaga, 10; Moogoon, 18, Newman's, 20; M'Donald's, 2; Lucas, 16, Yambercollie, 5; Goondiwindi, 7. Total, 198 miles.

- DALBY AND ST. GEORGE. Mail Route. Dalby to Loudon, Weranga, and Marmudah, 44 miles; thence to Deep Crossing, 19; Middle Creek, 12; Tartha, 15; Southwood, 19; Bendee, 15; Kincora, 15; Brushy Park, 6; Cooroora, 12; North Ingleton, 11; Coomrith, 12; Canmaroo, 15; South Teelba, 18; Minton, 12, Kooroon, 10; Hollymount, 15; Thomby, 19; St. George, 35. Total, 304 miles.

- MARYLAND (N.S.W.) AND TENTERFIELD (N.S.W.) Maryland to Ruby Creek, N.S.W., 7 miles; thence to Wilson's Downfall (p. o.) N.S.W., 13; Tenterfield, 22. Total, 42 miles.

- MILES AND TAROOM.—Mail Route. Miles to Christianburg Saw Mills, 3 miles; thence to Juandah, 47; Rochdale, 15; Carrabah, 13; Lilyvile, 7; Taroom, 5. Total, 90 miles. Carrabah to Bungaban, 15 miles. Total, 105 miles.

- MILES AND SURAT. Mail Route. Miles to Tieryboo, 20 miles; thence to Condamine, 4; Myall Grove, Yulabilla, 15; Blythland, 15; Undullah, 16; Beta, 10; Yulabilla, 7; Coalbar (Haas), 18; Ladas Downs, 2; Murilla (Bell and Sons), 16; Warkon, 5; Combarngo, 10; Noorindoo, 4; Surat, 15. Total, 157 miles. On the south side of the Condamine the route is as follows :—Condamine to Bin Bin, 8 miles; thence to Morabie, 20; thence to Waundungal, 12; thence to Warkon, 10; thence to Bingi, 12; thence to Noorindoo, 6; thence to Surat, 16; total, 84 miles.

- MITCHELL DOWNS AND WARRENVILLE. Mail Route. Mitchell Downs to Donnybrook, 35; thence to Forest Vale, 14; Redford, 40; Warrenville, 10. Total, 99 miles.

- MITCHELL DOWNS AND WOOLERINA. Mail Route. Mitchell Downs to Salamis, 47; thence to Citheria, 6; Lusvale, 18; Tongy, 4; Grassmere, 30; Homboin, 3; Bindebango, 20; Bollon, 22; Tilquin, —; Mona, —; Woolerina, 36. Total, 186 miles.

- MITCHELL AND ST. GEORGE. Mail Route. Mitchell to Amby Junction, 27 miles; thence Claravale, 14; thence to Kilmorey, 10; Toolumbilla, 20; Womblebank, 10; Merivale, 20; Westgrove, 15; Rockvale, 6; ?atton Vale,

6, Glen Tullock, 6. Total, 125 miles. Copley Bros, and Annie Vale Station get their mails from Amby Junction; Perwell Station gets mail from Hillsborough; Rockwood from Bonna Vista.

- MITCHELL DOWNS AND GLEN TULLOCH. Mail Route. Mitchel Downs, via Waroonga, 18 miles; Claravale 14; thence to Kilmorey, 10; Toolumbilla, 20; Womblebank, 10; Merivale, 20; Westgrove, 15; Glen Tulloch, 18. Total, 125 miles.

- ROMA AND SURAT. Roma to Hope's Creek (Beaconsfield), Cooinda, thence via Fairview to Merino Downs, 22 miles; Rockybank, 7; Trinidad, 12; Sawmill, 2; Oberina. 5; Surat, 18. Total, 66 miles. Stations served by this route;—Coogoon on Coogoon Creek. 12 miles west of Rockybank; Urumble (Gogg's), 12 miles west of Coogoon and Dallally. Another Road. Roma to Brucedale, 22 miles; thence to Cattle Station, 10; Spring Grove, 13; Surat, 5.

- ROMA AND BALLAROO. Mail Route. Roma to Beaconsfield. 13 miles; Cooindra, 9, Merino Downs, 4; Belleview, 2; Emerald Bank. 7; Rocky Bank, 4; Stratton, 6; Coogoon, 15; Balaroo, 15. Total, 75 miles.

- ROMA AND BRUCEDALE. Distance, 22 Miles.

- ROMA AND TAROOM. Roma to Euthella, 10 miles; thence to Gulberamunda, 13; Myall Downs, 23; Mount Hutton, 20; Springwater, 15; Pony Hills, 10; Baroondah, 22; Hornet Brook, 16; Euroombah, 12; Llandillo, 16; Bauhinia, Vale, 14; Taroom, 10. Total, 170 miles.

- ROMA AND FAIR CREEK. Mail Route. Yingerbay, 20 miles; Fair Creek, 18½. Total, 38½ miles.

- ROMA AND QUIBET. Roma, via Hope's Creek, Beaconsfield, Cooindra, to Merino Downs, 22 miles; thence, via Bellevue to Rockybank, 7; Coogoon, 15; Ballaroo, 12; Quibet, 20. Total, 76 miles.

- ROMA AND GORDON PARK. Roma Downs, 5 miles; Richmond, 4; Laurestein, 2; Waterview, 4; Mount Pleasant, 1; Fairview, 2; Glencoe, 2; Fairfield, 8; Gordon Park, 10. Total, 38 miles.

- ST. GEORGE AND HEBEL. Mail Route. St. George Post Office to Old and New Boombah, 7½ miles; thence to Police Barracks, 18; Boah, 15; Dirranbandi, 14; Currawildi, 1½; Booligal, 22; Nee Nee, 8; Hebei, 12. Total, 98 miles. Curriwillinghi Station, 3 miles from Hebel. Cur-riwillinghi is about 4 miles this side of the border. The nearest New South Wales post office is Goodooga on the Bree River, about 20 miles dis-tant from Curriwillinghi and 8 miles from Brenda. From Cowildi to Dareel on the Surat and Yarrowa line, the distance is about 60 miles. An-other route from St. George to Curriwillinghi is as follows : —St. George to Doondi, 21 miles; thence to Whyenbah public house, 15; Boah, 1; Currawildi, 15; Boondah (Ballandool River), 30; Curriwillinghi, 12. From Currawildi to Eyuranbah, the distance is 18 miles; thence to Bienherri, 4; Eyuranbah (New South Wales), 20; Noolawal, 2½; Angledool, 1—the latter station being about 15 miles to the eastward of Curriwillinghi. Toothar West is about 25 miles from Whyenbah, on the west side of the Culgoa River; Toothar East on the east side of that river. From Tooth to Murra the distance is 13 miles; thence to Mogangulla, —; Minnumningdi, 8; and from thence the road leads to Berga, on the 29th parallel. Berga is about 25 miles S.W of Curriwillinghi. Walgett Post Office (N.S.W.) is about 96 miles from Curriwillinghi, in a southern direction, at the junction of the Naomi and Barwon Rivers … Curriwillinghi to Goodooga, 26 miles; thence to Brenda, 8; where it meets the Brewarrina and Bourke mail.

- ST. GEORGE AND CUNNAMULLA. Mail Route to Bollon. St. George to Wondit Dam, 20 miles; thence to Boolba Waterhole, 20; Uhr's Waterhole, 26; Bollon Post Office, 20; Mungallala Creek, 10; Theodore Tank, 20; Nebine Creek, 15; Shamrock Wells, 18; Widgeegoara Creek. 26; Blue's Tank, 14; Cunnamulla, 14. Total, 203 miles.

- ST. GEORGE AND BOLLON. Via 20, 40, and 65 Mile Bores. Mail Route.—80 Miles.

- ST. GEORGE AND MUNGINDI, N.S.W. Mail Route. St. George to Minimi, 6 miles; thence to Nindigully, 28; Bullamon, 24; Dareel, 17; Mungindi post office, Queensland, 15; Mungindi post office, N.S.W., 1. Total, 91 miles. Both the Mungindi post offices are on the borders of N.S.W. and Queensland, separated by the Barwon River.

- STANTHORPE AND NUNDUBBERMERE. Mail Route. —15 Miles.

- STANTHORPE AND TEXAS. Mail Route (Coach). Stanthorpe to Mallow, 11 miles; Pikedale R. 0., 10; Terrica,

16; Dowling's, 3½; Warroo, 6½; Brush Creek, 13; Copmanhurst, 16; Texas Flat, 3; Texas P. and T. Office, I. Total, 80 miles.

- STANTHORPE AND PIKEDALE REEFS. Distance, 25 Miles.
- STANTHORPE AND WILSON'S DOWNFALL, NEW SOUTH WALES. Mail Route. Stanthorpe to Kyoomba Post Office, 4 miles; thence to Sugarloaf, 5; Wilson's Downfall, N.S.W., 4. Total, 13 miles.
- TOOWOOMBA AND DRAYTON. Mail Route. —Distance, 4 Miles. TOOWOOMBA AND CHARLEVILLE. Railway. Mail Route. Toowoom-ba to Gowrie Junction, 8 miles; thence to Gowrie railway station, 4; Oakey Creek railway station, 6; Jondaryan railway station, 9; Bowenville, 8; Blaxland's Siding, 13; Dalby, 3; Macalister, 15; Warra, 13; Chinchilla, 22; Miles, 28; Paddy's Creek, 4|; Dulacca,
- 22|; Channing's, 14; Yeulba, 9; Blythedale, 7; Roma, 20; Bungeworgorai, 16; Hodson, 6; Brinsop, 9; Muckadilla, 6; Amby, 12; East Mitchell, 14; Mitchell, 1; Womallala, 10; Mugallala, 19; Dulbydilla, 10; Morven, 16; Augathella, 15; Charleville, 42. Total, 382 miles.
- TOOWOOMBA AND MIDDLE RIDGE. Mail Route. —Distance, 3 Miles.
- TOOWOOMBA AND WALLANGARRA. Railway. Mail Route. Toowoomba to Meringandan, 3 miles; thence to Gowrie Junction receiving of-fice, 5; Williams's Camp, 6; Westbrook Crossing. 3; Cambooya post office, 8; Greenmount, 7; King's Creek, 9; Clifton Post Office, 2; Elphinstone, 2; Hendon (for Allora), 9; Deuchar's Crossing, 3; Lyndhurst Road, 7; Warwick, 2; East Warwick, 2; Cherry Gully, 18; Maryland, 4; Dalveen, 3; Stanthorpe, 14; Wallangarra, 25. Total, 131 miles.
- YULEBA AND ST. GEORGE. Yuleba to Mongul, 8 miles; thence to Combarngo, 16; Murinda, 15; Springrove, 13; Surat 5; Talavera to Weribone, 12; Donga, 25; Waroo, 12; Borgorah, 30; St. George Township (post office), 6 miles. Total 142 miles.

Reference List

1852 DOMESTIC INTELLIGENCE.', The Moreton Bay Courier (Brisbane, Qld. : 1846 - 1861), 1 May, p. 3. , viewed 06 Mar 2022, http://nla.gov.au/nla.news- article3712351. The National Library of Australia.

1856 'ADVERTISING', Bendigo Advertiser (Vic. : 1855 - 1918), 23 May, p. 3. , viewed 14 Nov 2020, http://nla.gov.au/nla.news-article88050197 The National Library.

1856 'DRAYTON', The North Australian, Ipswich and General Advertiser (Ipswich, Qld. : 1856 - 1862), 12 August, p. 3. , viewed 04 Mar 2022, http://nla.gov.au/nla.news-article788498041856. The National Library of Australia.

1858 'MORETON BAY.', The Age (Melbourne, Vic. : 1854 - 1954), 5 April, p. 6. , viewed 03 Mar 2022, http://nla.gov.au/nla.news- article1548585001858. The National Library of Australia.

1859 'ADJOURNED LICENSES MEETING.', The Darling Downs Gazette and General Advertiser (Toowoomba, Qld. : 1858 - 1880), 5 May, p. 3. , viewed 04 Mar 2022, http://nla.gov.au/nla.news-article75524447. The National Library of Australia.

1859 'CONVEYANCE OF MAILS.', New South Wales Government Gazette (Sydney, NSW : 1832 - 1900), 14 October, p. 2258. , viewed 21 Feb 2022, http://nla.gov.au/nla.news-article228602182 1859. The National Library of Australia.

1859 'CONVEYANCE OF MAILS.', The North Australian, Ipswich and General Advertiser (Ipswich, Qld. : 1856 - 1862), 27 September, p. 3. , viewed 09 Mar 2022, http://nla.gov.au/nla.news-article77429882. The National Library of Australia.

1861 'CONVEYANCE OF MAILS.', The Courier (Brisbane, Qld. : 1861 - 1864), 16 September, p. 6. , viewed 21 Feb 2022, http://nla.gov.au/nla.news- article46010341861. The National Library of Australia.

1863 'ATLAS OF AUSTRALASIA.', Proeschel, Fredrick (1809-1870), Publisher Brown & Slight, Emerald Hill [Vic.] viewed 26 January 2022 Published Emerald Hill [Vic.] : Brown & Slight, [1863] Call number MAP RaA 13 http://nla.gov.au/nla.obj-230987456. The National Library of Australia.

1894 'THE TOOWOOMBA CHRONICLE.', The Sydney Mail and New South Wales Advertiser (NSW : 1871 - 1912), 17 November, p. 1016. , viewed 15 July 2025, http://nla.gov.au/nla.news-article162836399. The National Library of Australia.

1864 'DALBY', The Darling Downs Gazette and General Advertiser (Toowoomba, Qld. : 1858 - 1880), 24 December, p. 3. , viewed 09 Mar 2022, http://nla.gov.au/nla.news-article75512180. The National Library of Australia.

1865 'DALBY', The Brisbane Courier (Qld. : 1864 - 1933), 27 March, p. 3. , viewed 09 Mar 2022, http://nla.gov.au/nla.news-article1270094. The National Library of Australia.

1866 'COBB AND CO'S COACHES.', The Queenslander (Brisbane, Qld. : 1866 - 1939), 2 June, p. 4. , viewed 23 Feb 2022, http://nla.gov.au/nla.news- article20307846. The National Library of Australia.

1866 'ADVERTISING', Dalby Herald and Western Queensland Advertiser (Qld. : 1866 - 1879), 4 October, p. 1. , viewed 04 Jun 2024, http://nla.gov.au/nla.news-article215448519

1866 'ADVERTISING', The Darling Downs Gazette and General Advertiser (Toowoomba, Qld. : 1858 - 1880), 6 March, p. 4. , viewed 03 Jun 2024, http://nla.gov.au/nla.news-article75516687

1866 'ADVERTISING', The Darling Downs Gazette and General Advertiser (Toowoomba, Qld. : 1858 - 1880), 31 March, p. 4. , viewed 03 Jun 2024, http://nla.gov.au/nla.news-article75516898

1866 'CLASSIFIED ADVERTISING', The Brisbane Courier (Qld. : 1864 - 1933), 21 February, p. 1. , viewed 04 Jun 2024, http://nla.gov.au/nla.news-article1262907

1866 'TOOWOOMBA POLICE COURT.', The Toowoomba Chronicle and Queensland Advertiser (Qld. : 1861 - 1875), 15 August, p. 2. , viewed 03 Jun 2024, http://nla.gov.au/nla.news-article212786301

1867 'ADVERTISING', The Darling Downs Gazette and General Advertiser (Toowoomba, Qld. : 1858 - 1880), 19 March, p. 4, viewed 09 Mar 2022, http://nla.gov.au/nla.news-article75518977. The National Library of Australia.

1867 'CONDAMINE', Dalby Herald and Western Queensland Advertiser (Qld. : 1866 - 1879), 2 November, p. 3. , viewed 07 Aug 2021, http://nla.gov.au/nla.news-article215452054. The National Library of Australia.

1867 'MAIL BETWEEN TOOWOOMBA AND HIGHFIELDS.', The Toowoomba Chronicle and Queensland Advertiser (Qld. : 1861 - 1875), 9 November, p. 2. , viewed 10 Sep 2021, http://nla.gov.au/nla.news-article212782642. The National Library of Australia.

1867 'CLASSIFIED ADVERTISING', The Brisbane Courier (Qld. : 1864 - 1933), 25 October, p. 1. , viewed 04 Jun 2024, http://nla.gov.au/nla.news-article1288110

1867 'TOOWOOMBA.', The Brisbane Courier (Qld. : 1864 - 1933), 20 March, p. 3. , viewed 04 Jun 2024, http://nla.gov.au/nla.news-article1281741

1868 'CLASSIFIED ADVERTISING', The Queenslander (Brisbane, Qld. : 1866 - 1939), 4 January, p. 1. , viewed 04 Jun 2024, http://nla.gov.au/nla.news-article20316702

1869 'CONSEYANCE OF MALIS FOR 1870.', Warwick Examiner and Times (Qld. : 1867 - 1919), 11 December, p. 2. , viewed 26 May 2021, http://nla.gov.au/nla.news-article82098758. The National Library of Australia.

1870 'DALBY', The Queenslander (Brisbane, Qld. : 1866 - 1939), 3 December, p. 10. , viewed 25 Mar 2022, http://nla.gov.au/nla.news- article27263678. The National Library of Australia.

1871 'ADVERTISING', Dalby Herald and Western Queensland Advertiser (Qld. : 1866 - 1879), 1 April, p. 1. , viewed 04 Jun 2024, http://nla.gov.au/nla.news-article215603027

1871 'TELEGRAPHIC.', Maryborough Chronicle, Wide Bay and Burnett Advertiser (Qld. : 1860 - 1947), 22 August, p. 2. , viewed 04 Jun 2024, http://nla.gov.au/nla.news-article148532731

1873 'CONDAMINE', Queensland Times, Ipswich Herald and General Advertiser (Qld. : 1861 - 1908), 19 April, p. 4. , viewed 07 Aug 2021, http://nla.gov.au/nla.news-article122562489 The National Library of Australia.

1873 'CONDAMINE', The Darling Downs Gazette and General Advertiser (Toowoomba, Qld. : 1858 - 1880), 9 April, p. 3. , viewed 07 Aug 2021, http://nla.gov.au/nla.news-article77086183. The National Library of Australia.

1875 'COBB & CO.', Gympie Times and Mary River Mining Gazette (Qld. : 1868 - 1919), 5 May, p. 4. , viewed 10 Dec 2020, http://nla.gov.au/nla.news-article168911735 Page identifier http://nla.gov.au/nla.news-page20144689 The National Library of Australia.

1876 'CHARLEVILLE TO DALBY PER COBB AND CO.'S COACH.', Western Star and Roma Advertiser (Qld. :

1875 - 1948), 22 January, p. 3. , viewed 11 Feb 2022, http://nla.gov.au/nla.news-article97420439. The National Library of Australia.

1878 'ADVERTISING' Toowoomba Chronicle and Darling Downs General Advertiser (Qld. : 1875 - 1902) 24 December 1878: 4. Web. 4 Jun 2024 http://nla.gov.au/nla.news-article217700712

1878 'BRISBANE.', Toowoomba Chronicle and Darling Downs General Advertiser (Qld. : 1875 - 1902), 6 June, p. 4. , viewed 04 Jun 2024, http://nla.gov.au/nla.news-article217699064

1878 'CLASSIFIED ADVERTISING', The Brisbane Courier (Qld. : 1864 - 1933), 27 February, p. 6. , viewed 14 July 2025, http://nla.gov.au/nla.news-article1370274

1879 'COAL BETWEEN DALBY AND ROMA.', Dalby Herald and Western Queensland Advertiser (Qld. : 1866 - 1879), 25 October, p. 4. , viewed 25 Feb 2022, http://nla.gov.au/nla.news-article215610275. The National Library of Australia.

1881 'A HOLIDAY RAMBLE ON THE YARRA TRACK.', Illustrated Australian News (Melbourne, Vic. : 1876 - 1889), viewed 26 Mar 2022, http://nla.gov.au/nla.news-article63185338. The National Library of Australia.

1892 'FUNNY THOUGHTS.', The Telegraph (Brisbane, Qld. : 1872 - 1947), 10 March, p. 5. , viewed 15 July 2025, http://nla.gov.au/nla.news-article174044947. The National Library of Australia.

1884 'BRISBANE HOUSE CLUB ASSOCIATION.', Queensland Figaro (Brisbane, Qld. : 1883 - 1885), 12 April, p. 18. , viewed 28 Feb 2023, http://nla.gov.au/nla.news-article83673476. The National Library of Australia.

1886 'FROM BRISBANE TO ADAVALE.', The Brisbane Courier (Qld. : 1864 - 1933), 3 May, p. 6. , viewed 16 Feb 2023, http://nla.gov.au/ nla.news-article4493939.

1894 'COBB AND CO.', The Sydney Mail and New South Wales Advertiser (NSW : 1871 - 1912), 17 November, p. 1016. , viewed 28 Feb 2023, http://nla.gov.au/nla.news-article162836401. The National Library of Australia.

1895 'A MARANOA REMINISCENCE.', Western Star and Roma Advertiser (Qld. : 1875 - 1948), 27 March, p. 3. , viewed 25 Feb 2022, http://nla.gov.au/nla.news-article97531075. The National Library of Australia.

1895 'COBB AND CO.', Windsor and Richmond Gazette (NSW : 1888 - 1971), 20 April, p. 9. , viewed 15 July 2025, http://nla.gov.au/nla.news-article66446598. The National Library of Australia.

1895 'GEOGRAPHIC HISTORY OF QUEENSLAND.', Meston, Archibald [online] Edmund Gregory Government Printer, Brisbane. Available at: https://espace.library.uq.edu.au The University of Queensland. [Accessed 7 Dec. 2020].

1895 'LOCAL AND GENERAL NEWS.', Queensland Times, Ipswich Herald and General Advertiser (Qld. : 1861 - 1908), 24 December, p. 4. , viewed 04 Jun 2024, http://nla.gov.au/nla.news-article130381828

1896 'COBB AND CO.', Wagga Wagga Advertiser (NSW : 1875 - 1910), 20 October, p. 4. , viewed 28 Feb 2023, http://nla.gov.au/nla.news- article101780141. The National Library of Australia.

1897 'COBB & CO.'S CATALOGUE OF HIGH CLASS VEHICLES.', One Search (State Library of Queensland), pp.1-28 bishop.slq.qld.gov.au, viewed 17 March 2021, Record number 997321704702061, 21111147640002061

1897 'COBB AND CO.', Weekly Times (Melbourne, Vic. : 1869 - 1954), 4 September, p. 5. (THE WEEKLY TIMES SPECIAL SHOW SUPPLEMENT), viewed 11 July 2025, http://nla.gov.au/nla.news-article221133626

1897 'THE BULLETIN', Vol. 18 No. 295 (6 Nov 1897) https://nla.gov.au/nla.obj-672369530/view?sectionId=nla.obj-686259017&searchTerm=%22and+the+music+of+the+big+bells%2C+as+they+let+the+horses+go%22&partId=nla.obj-672486810#page/n4/mode/1up

1897 'COBB AND CO.', The Grenfell Record and Lachlan District Advertiser (NSW : 1876 - 1951), 18 December, p. 2. , viewed 16 Dec 2021, http://nla.gov.au/nla.news-article117235941. The National Library of Australia.

1897 'FIRE AT CHARLEVILLE.', The Argus (Melbourne, Vic. : 1848 - 1957), 17 November, p. 5. , viewed 14 Aug 2021, http://nla.gov.au/nla.news- article9779445. The National Library of Australia.

1898 'MR. S. S. BASSETT'S VINEYARD.', The Queenslander (Brisbane, Qld. : 1866 - 1939), 10 September, p. 521. (Unknown), viewed 13 Feb 2023, http://nla.gov.au/nla.news-article20851204. National Library of Australia.

1901 'NORTHWARD TO THE SHED.', Worker (Brisbane, Qld. : 1890 - 1955), 27 April, p. 7. , viewed 15 July 2025, http://nla.gov.au/nla.news-article70830714. National Library of Australia.

1901 'A LARGE COACH.', Darling Downs Gazette (Qld. : 1881 - 1922), 12 August, p. 2. , viewed 14 Aug 2021, http://nla.gov.au/nla.news- article171560703. The National Library of Australia.

1901 'DEATH OF MR. JOHN WAGNER.', The Argus (Melbourne, Vic. : 1848 - 1957), 28 January, p. 7. , viewed 30 Sep 2021, http://nla.gov.au/nla.news-article10532005. The National Library of Australia.

1902 'COBB AND CO.'S COACHES', The Sydney Morning Herald (NSW : 1842 - 1954), 16 May, p. 6. , viewed 29 Mar 2022, http://nla.gov.au/nla.news-article14466347. The National Library of Australia.

1902 'COBB AND CO.'S SHAREHOLDERS.', The Brisbane Courier (Qld. : 1864 - 1933), 29 May, p. 4. , viewed 16 Dec 2021, http://nla.gov.au/nla.news- article19190671. The National Library of Australia.

1902 'COBB AND COMPANY.', Western Mail (Perth, WA : 1885 - 1954), 17 May, p. 23. , viewed 22 Feb 2022, http://nla.gov.au/nla.news- article33217077. The National Library of Australia.

1902 'MY LIFE IN MANY STATES AND IN FOREIGN LANDS.', Train, George Francis. Pp. Xxi. 340. D. Appleton: New York. SR 910.4 T768. The National Library of Australia.

1904 'THE DAYS OF COBB & CO.', The Hillston Spectator and Lachlan River Advertiser (NSW : 1898 - 1952), 4 March, p. 4. , viewed 15 July 2025, http://nla.gov.au/nla.news-article131373737. The National Library of Australia.

1904 'ROMA BORE GAS.', The Brisbane Courier (Qld. : 1864 - 1933), 29 April, p. 4. , viewed 14 July 2025, http://nla.gov.au/nla.news-article19278013. The National Library of Australia.

1904-1908 'GROOM'S DARLING DOWNS BOOK ALMANAC AND TOOWOOMBA ... local business directory for 1902, pp. 206-210. National Library of Australia. https://nla.gov.au/nla.obj-3022037874/view?sectionId=nla.obj-3023736882&searchTerm=roma+gas&partId=nla.obj-3022065969#page/n4/mode/ 1up

1905 'HODGSON', Western Star and Roma Advertiser (Qld. : 1875 - 1948), 22 February, p. 3. , viewed 22 Mar 2022, http://

nla.gov.au/nla.news- article97406592. The National Library of Australia.

1906 'OIL AT ROMA.', Newcastle Morning Herald and Miners' Advocate (NSW : 1876 - 1954), 23 June, p. 11. , viewed 04 Aug 2021, http://nla.gov.au/nla.news-article136228176 The National Library of Australia.

1907 'JAMES RUTHERFORD.', Truth (Brisbane, Qld. : 1900 - 1954), 22 December, p. 11. , viewed 11 Aug 2021, http://nla.gov.au/nla.news- article206486048 The National Library of Australia.

1908 'MINERAL OIL AT ROMA.', The Bundaberg Mail and Burnett Advertiser (Qld. : 1892 - 1917), 28 October, p. 2. , viewed 14 Aug 2021, http://nla.gov.au/nla.news-article215292944. The National Library of Australia.

1909 'MOTOR BUGGIES.', Singleton Argus (NSW : 1880 - 1954), 20 July, p. 2. , viewed 22 Dec 2021, http://nla.gov.au/nla.news-article76903393. The National Library of Australia.

1910 'MOTOR NOTES.', Punch (Melbourne, Vic. : 1900 - 1918; 1925), 28 April, p. 35. , viewed 22 Dec 2021, http://nla.gov.au/nla.news-article176545978. The National Library of Australia.

1911 'A LINK WITH COBB AND CO.'S COACHES.', Queensland Times (Ipswich, Qld. : 1909 - 1954), 28 September, p. 4. (DAILY), viewed 29 Mar 2022, http://nla.gov.au/nla.news-article112041629. The National Library.

1911 'AN HISTORICAL MAGAZINE.' The Age (Melbourne, Vic. : 1854 - 1954) Web. Viewed 10 Dec 2020 . Page identifier http://nla.gov.au/nla.news- page18563235 The National Library of Australia.

1911 'AUSTRALIAN PIONEER.', Darling Downs Gazette (Qld. : 1881 - 1922), 19 September, p. 6. , viewed 20 Feb 2022, http://nla.gov.au/nla.news- article180625010 1911. The National Library of Australia.

1912 'LAND OFFICE APPOINTMENT.', Western Star and Roma Advertiser (Qld. : 1875 - 1948), 2 November, p. 2. , viewed 25 Mar 2022, http://nla.gov.au/nla.news-article98155678. The National Library of Australia.

1912 'MESSRS. COBB AND CO.', Morning Bulletin (Rockhampton, Qld. : 1878 - 1954), 29 April, p. 6. , viewed 16 Dec 2021, http://nla.gov.au/nla.news- article53266882. The National Library of Australia.

1914 'SALE OF QUEENSLAND SHEEP PROPERTY.', Leader (Orange, NSW : 1899 - 1945), 2 February, p. 2. , viewed 14 July 2025, http://nla.gov.au/nla.news-article119895409. The National Library of Australia.

1914 'DARGAL CREEK.', Western Star and Roma Advertiser (Qld. : 1875 - 1948), 25 April, p. 3. , viewed 25 Mar 2022, http://nla.gov.au/nla.news- article98158905 1914. The National Library of Australia.

1915 'DARGAL CREEK.', Western Star and Roma Advertiser (Qld. : 1875 - 1948), 14 July, p. 3. , viewed 25 Mar 2022, http://nla.gov.au/nla.news- article98165461. The National Library of Australia.

1915 'FIRE IN ROMA.', The Telegraph (Brisbane, Qld. : 1872 - 1947), 10 May, p. 2. (Second Edition), viewed 12 Feb 2023, http://nla.gov.au/nla.news-article176931210. National Library of Australia.

1915 'NEW RAILWAYS.', The Sydney Stock and Station Journal (NSW : 1896 - 1924), 17 December, p. 8. , viewed 20 Feb 2022, http://nla.gov.au/nla.news- article125905018. The National Library of Australia.

1916 'FIFTY YEARS AGO.', Queensland Times (Ipswich, Qld. : 1909 - 1954), 25 March, p. 12. (DAILY.), viewed 04 Jun 2024, http://nla.gov.au/nla.news-article113137775

1917 'BLAZE AT ROMA.', Toowoomba Chronicle (Qld. : 1917 - 1922), 15 December, p. 4. , viewed 12 Feb 2023, http://nla.gov.au/nla.news- article252880521. National Library of Australia.

1917 'COACHING IN AUSTRALIA : a history of the coaching firm of Cobb & Co. with guide to the present coaching routes in Queensland.', Lees,William. Brisbane: Carter-Watson Co., Record Number 996938114702061, 21113295690002061 Available at: [Accessed 1 Oct. 2020]. Print. State Library South Bank Collection. (Coaching in Australia : a history of the coaching firm of Cobb & Co. with guide to the present coaching routes in Queensland, 1917) * Note reference to the book Coaching in Australia in 1917 in 'The Genesis of Cobb & Co', The Western Champion and General Advertiser for the Central-Western Districts (Barcaldine, Qld. : 1892 - 1922), 15 September, p. 11. , viewed 18 Mar 2021, http://nla.gov.au/nla.news-article77790761 and in 'Cobb and Co.', 1917, The Queenslander (Brisbane, Qld. : 1866 - 1939), 1 September, p. 3. , viewed 20 Apr 2021, http://nla.gov.au/nla.news-page2539743. (Coaching in Australia, W. Lees, 1917)

1917 'THE GENESIS OF COBB & CO', The Western Champion and General Advertiser for the Central-Western Districts (Barcaldine, Qld. : 1892 - 1922), 15 September, p. 11. , viewed 04 Jun 2024, http://nla.gov.au/nla.news-article77790761

1918 'DRAYTON DEVIATION ACCIDENT', The Toowoomba Chronicle (Qld. : 1902 - 1922), 25 May, p. 6. , viewed 11 July 2025, http://nla.gov.au/nla.news-article252973129

1919 'FIRE AT ROMA.', Warwick Daily News (Qld. : 1919 -1954), 11 March, p. 4. , viewed 12 Feb 2023, http://nla.gov.au/nla.news- article175736150. National Library of Australia.

1920 'ADVERTISING', Western Star and Roma Advertiser (Qld. : 1875 - 1948), 7 July, p. 2. , viewed 22 Mar 2022, http://nla.gov.au/nla.news- article98182681. The National Library of Australia.

1920 'ADVERTISING', Western Star and Roma Advertiser (Qld. : 1875 - 1948), 18 August, p. 4. , viewed 22 Mar 2022, http://nla.gov.au/nla.news- article98183233. The National Library of Australia.

1920 'COBB & CO.'S COACH FACTORY.', The Queenslander (Brisbane, Qld. : 1866 - 1939), 25 December, p. 16. , viewed 14 Aug 2021, http://nla.gov.au/nla.news-article25324633. The National Library of Australia.

1920 'COBB AND CO.'S CHARLEVILLE FACTORY.', The Brisbane Courier (Qld. : 1864 - 1933), 26 November, p. 4. , viewed 11 Feb 2022, http://nla.gov.au/nla.news-article20460047. The National Library of Australia.

1920 'COBB AND COMPANY.', Toowoomba Chronicle (Qld. : 1917 - 1922), 21 December, p. 5. , viewed 14 Aug 2021, http://nla.gov.au/nla.news-article253192658. The National Library of Australia.

1920 'EXIT COBB AND CO.', Daily Advertiser (Wagga Wagga, NSW : 1911 - 1954), 20 December, p. 2. , viewed 23 Aug 2021, http://nla.gov.au/nla.news-article142294696. The National Library of Australia.

1922 'ADVERTISING', Western Star and Roma Advertiser (Qld. : 1875 - 1948), 1 July, p. 3. , viewed 25 Mar 2022, http://nla.gov.au/nla.news- article98187562. The National Library of Australia.

1922 'COBB AND CO.', Morning Bulletin (Rockhampton, Qld. : 1878 - 1954), 20 June, p. 13. , viewed 06 Aug 2021, http://nla.gov.au/nla.news- article54018319. The National Library of Australia.

1922 'COBB AND CO.', Queensland Times (Ipswich, Qld. : 1909 - 1954), 4 November, p. 12. (DAILY.), viewed 16 Dec 2021, http://nla.gov.au/nla.news-article111128826. The National Library of Australia.

1922 'GERMANS DEPRESSED.', Western Star and Roma Advertiser (Qld. : 1875 - 1948), 22 April, p. 2. , viewed 22 Mar 2022, http://nla.gov.au/nla.news- article98072081. The National Library of Australia.

1923 'COBB AND CO.', Balonne Beacon (St. George, Qld. : 1909 - 1954), 20 October, p. 4. , viewed 13 Aug 2021, http://nla.gov.au/nla.news- article218938533. The National Library of Australia.

1923 'FOUNDERS OF BRISBANE.', The Queenslander (Brisbane, Qld. : 1866 - 1939), 7 April, p. 11. , viewed 22 Feb 2022, http://nla.gov.au/nla.news- article226420351923. The National Library of Australia.

1923 'MONEY MARKET SEARCHLIGHT.', The Telegraph (Brisbane, Qld. : 1872 - 1947), 29 November, p. 9. , viewed 21 Dec 2021, http://nla.gov.au/nla.news-article180473661. The National Library of Australia.

1923 'GLIMPSES OF IPSWICH HISTORY.', Queensland Times (Ipswich, Qld. : 1909 - 1954), 24 October, p. 9. (DAILY.), viewed 04 Jun 2024, http://nla.gov.au/nla.news-article125408894

1924 'AN OLD-TIME INN.', The Brisbane Courier (Qld. : 1864 - 1933), 5 July, p. 6. , viewed 03 Mar 2022, http://nla.gov.au/nla.news- article207387451924. The National Library of Australia.

1924 'EXIT COBB'S.', The Southern Mail (Bowral, NSW : 1889 - 1954), 5 September, p. 3. , viewed 21 May 2021, http://nla.gov.au/nla.news-article114063569. The National Library of Australia.

1924 'LAST COACH.', The Sydney Morning Herald (NSW : 1842 - 1954), 4 September, p. 8. , viewed 25 Mar 2022, http://nla.gov.au/nla.news- article16175625. The National Library of Australia.

1924 'MEMORIES OF A PIONEER.', The Brisbane Courier (Qld. : 1864 - 1933), 21 June, p. 18. , viewed 03 Jun 2024, http://nla.gov.au/nla.news-article20734355

1925 'BIRTH OF QUEENSLAND.', The Daily Mail (Brisbane, Qld. : 1903 - 1926), 6 December, p. 26. , viewed 24 May 2021, http://nla.gov.au/nla.news- article217639463. The National Library of Australia.

1925 'BRISBANE EXHIBITION.', Cairns Post (Qld. : 1909 - 1954), 14 August, p. 3. , viewed 11 Feb 2023, http://nla.gov.au/nla.news-article40506366.The National Library of Australia.

1925 'COBB'S COACHES.', The Brisbane Courier (Qld. : 1864 - 1933), 17 January, p. 17. , viewed 18 May 2021, http://nla.gov.au/nla.news- article20898443. The National Library of Australia.

1926 'MITCHELL CHILDREN'S BALL.', The Brisbane Courier (Qld. : 1864 - 1933), 7 July, p. 22. , viewed 05 Apr 2022, http://nla.gov.au/nla.news- article21035814. The National Library of Australia.

1926 'NOT FOR QUEENSLAND.', The Daily Mail (Brisbane, Qld. : 1903; 1916 - 1926), 3 August, p. 14. , viewed 10 July 2025, http://nla.gov.au/nla.news-article220656676

1927 'HODGSON', Western Star and Roma Advertiser (Qld. : 1875 - 1948), 14 May, p. 2. , viewed 22 Mar 2022, http://nla.gov.au/nla.news-article98027839 1927. The National Library of Australia.

1927 'ORIGINAL VERSE.', Maryborough Chronicle, Wide Bay and Burnett Advertiser (Qld. : 1860 - 1947), 11 July, p. 6. , viewed 13 July 2025, http://nla.gov.au/nla.news-article150980388. The National Library of Australia.

1928 'ROMA.', The Toowoomba Chronicle and Darling Downs Gazette (Qld. : 1922 - 1965), 27 August, p. 9. , viewed 14 July 2025, http://nla.gov.au/nla.news-article254050127. The National Library of Australia.

1929 'AERIAL BUSINESS TRIP TO ROMA.', The Brisbane Courier (Qld. : 1864 - 1933), 30 January, p. 17. , viewed 05 Apr 2022, http://nla.gov.au/nla.news-article21371423. The National Library of Australia.

1929 'COBB AND CO.'S COACHING DAYS: GOLOURFUL PAGE OF HISTORY CLOSED.', Sunday Mail (Brisbane, Qld. : 1926 - 1954), 30 June, p. 23. , viewed 16 Dec 2021, http://nla.gov.au/nla.news-article97696763. The National Library of Australia.

1931 'BLAZE AT ROMA.', The West Australian (Perth, WA : 1879 - 1954), 3 January, p. 6. , viewed 12 Feb 2023, http://nla.gov.au/nla.news- article33006402. National Library of Australia.

1931 'NO TITLE', Sydney Mail (NSW : 1912 - 1938), 28 October, p. 6. , viewed 13 July 2025, http://nla.gov.au/nla.news-article159794158. National Library of Australia.

1936 'ADVERTISING', Western Star and Roma Advertiser (Qld. : 1875 - 1948), 15 August, p. 3. , viewed 01 Apr 2022, http://nla.gov.au/nla.news- article98110911. The National Library of Australia.

1936 'OBITUARY. MR. H. J. JOHNSON.', Western Star and Roma Advertiser (Qld. : 1875 - 1948), 8 August, p. 2. , viewed 22 Mar 2022, http://nla.gov.au/nla.news-article98110789. The National Library of Australia.

1939 'COBB AND CO.', The World's News (Sydney, NSW : 1901 - 1955), 29 July, p. 45. , viewed 18 May 2021, http://nla.gov.au/nla.news- article131492264. The National Library of Australia.

1946 'FAMILY NOTICES', The Telegraph (Brisbane, Qld. : 1872 - 1947), 28 December, p. 4. (STUMPS SCORES), viewed 22 Mar 2022, http://nla.gov.au/nla.news-article187253844. The National Library of Australia.

1946 'OBITUARY MR. JONATHAN KEEGAN', Western Star and Roma Advertiser (Qld. : 1875 - 1948), 3 May, p. 5. , viewed 22 Mar 2022, http://nla.gov.au/nla.news-article98202234. The National Library of Australia.

1949 'COBB AND CO.', Balonne Beacon (St. George, Qld. : 1909 - 1954), 6 January, p. 4. , viewed 18 May 2021, http://nla.gov.au/nla.news- article215366040. The National Library of Australia.

1954 'HOSTEL FUNDS GET STIMULUS', Western Star (Roma) (Toowoomba, Qld. : 1948 - 1954), 14 December, p. 1. , viewed 14 July 2025, http://nla.gov.au/nla.news-article97560165. The National Library of Australia.

Index

Accident 30, 76, 77, 93
Adams and Co. 9, 10
Adavale 23, 109, 117, 118, 119, 140
Adelaide-street, Brisbane 30
Aerial mail service 110
Albert-street, Brisbane 28, 30, 118, 131
Albury 10
Alford, T. 41
Alice Downs 29, 57
Amby 44, 76, 89, 108, 140, 141
Amby Downs 76, 108,
American Telegraph Line of Coaches 10
Amity Point 27
Anthony Blake, 22
Aramac 28, 117
Artesian bore, Roma 73
Aubathalla 11
Augathella 44, 109, 117, 120, 140, 141
A. W. Robertson 10, 21, 25
Ayrshire Downs 117
Bail Up 77
Bainbilla 56
Ballone 55
Balonne River 56
Barnes, Hyram 28, 30, 75
Barringun 117
Bassett, Samuel 90
Bathurst 6, 10, 11, 13, 22, 109, 117, 125, 134
Beenleigh 28, 118
Bendemere 57, 139
Bendigo 10, 21
Beringa 56
Beringa Creek 56
Big Bingy 56
Billabongs 109
Bindango 78, 89, 108, 139
Bingie 55
Blackall 57, 109, 110, 117, 140
Black's Waterholes 107
Blake, Anthony 22
Blake, Arthur 10
Blaxland's Siding 44, 141
Blythedale 44, 55, 56, 77, 141
Blyth's Creek 71
Bollon 117, 140, 141

Bolton 57
Bombala 12
Booligal 22, 141
Boulia 117
Bourke 8, 9, 10, 12, 13, 22, 117, 132, 141
Bourke-street, Melbourne 9, 12, 22
Bowen 28, 29, 42, 77, 140
Bowen Downs 29
Bowen, Sir George 28
Bowen-street, Roma 77
Bowenvale 42
Bradley's farm 107
Bradley, W. 21
Braystone 56
Brinsop 44, 141
Brisbane 4, 6, 7, 10, 12, 19, 22, 25, 26, 27, 28, 29, 30, 31, 32, 33, 34, 35, 36, 37, 41, 42, 44, 45, 55, 56, 57, 72, 73, 75, 76, 77, 83, 84, 85, 89, 90, 107, 109, 110, 117, 118, 126, 131, 136, 137, 138
Brisbane River alligator 30
Brisbane (Scotland) 27
Brisbane, Sir Thomas 25, 27, 29
Brunig, R. 21
Buckinguy Station 11
Bulloo Creek 29
Bull's Head Inn, Drayton 41
Bundaberg 12
Bundamba 28
Bungeworgorai 44, 71, 72, 99, 139, 141
Bungil Creek 71, 72
Burdekin 29
Burketown 29
Burnett, J. C. 41
Burrenbella 11
Burren Junction 12
Bush Inn, Roma 74
Calandoon 55
Caledonian Hotel, Dalby 131
Cambooya 43, 141
Canal Creek 55, 137, 138
Canningtown 42
Cape Cod 10
Carrangarra, 29
Casey, Judge 12

Casino 55
Chambers, W. 9
Channing 44, 71, 141
Charleville 4, 6, 7, 23, 29, 44, 56, 57, 72, 75, 77, 88, 106, 107, 109, 110, 111, 112, 113, 114, 115, 116, 117, 118, 125, 126, 128, 140, 141
Charley's Creek 76
Charters Towers 28, 117, 118
Chinchilla 44, 118, 138, 141
Clark's Creek, Hodgson 88, 90, 92, 94
Clermont 111, 117, 118
Cloncurry 110, 117, 120, 121
Coal 11, 71, 72, 83
Cobb and Co.'s factories 15, 23, 30, 44, 109, 110, 125
Cobb & Co.'s stables 131
Cole, William (Scrammy Bill) 71
Commercial Bank of Sydney 56
Commercial Hotel, Roma 74
Commercial Hotel, Wallumbilla 57
Commercial Hotel, Warwick 131
Concord 10
Condamine 4, 7, 29, 43, 55, 56, 62, 71, 75, 76, 77, 108, 109, 131, 135, 137, 138, 139, 140
Condamine Arms Hotel 56
Connemarra 11
Coogoon 56, 140, 141
Cook, John 71
Cook's Hotel, Roma 71
Cooma 12
Coombing Park 11
Coonabarabran 12
Cork Station 117
Cornstalk Hotel, Roma 74
Court House Hotel, Roma 74
Crane and Roberts 9, 21, 22

Crawford, Connelly, and Co 10
Criterion Hotel, Dalby 131
Crook, James Elijah 9
Croydon 10
Cunnamulla 23, 57, 76, 109, 117, 141
Cunningham, Johnny 76
Cunningham's Gap 137
Cunningham-street, Dalby 60
Daandine 55, 109, 137, 138
Dagworth 117
Dalby 4, 7, 29, 30, 43, 44, 55, 56, 58, 59, 60, 71, 72, 75, 76, 77, 87, 107, 108, 109, 110, 117, 128, 131, 135, 137, 138, 140, 141
Dalby Herald 55
Dalrymple 29, 138
Dam mail-station 107
Dargal Creek 88, 89
Darling Downs 41, 42, 43, 52, 55, 72, 75, 76, 83, 125
Darling Downs Gazette 42
Davenport Downs 11, 22
Davies, Thomas 21
Dawson River 55
Dead Letter Office 28
Deepwater 77, 139
Deniliquin 22
Denkin, Alfred 22
Dogwood Creek 56
Downs Co-Operative Butter Factory 44
Downs Hotel, Warwick 131
Downs Inn, Drayton 41
Drayton 4, 7, 40, 41, 42, 43, 44, 45, 47, 50, 55, 129, 134, 135, 137
Drought 29, 70
Dubbo 11, 12
Dulacca 44, 76, 141
Dulbydilla 44, 117, 118, 141
Dynevor Downs 117
Echuca 22
Eddington 117
Edinburgh 27

Edinglassie 27
Elba 27
Elderslie 117
Emanuel King 9
Emerald 9, 28, 117, 141
Emu Creek 43
England 27, 28, 42, 56, 73, 75, 89, 90
Erskine, Governor 27
Eton Vale 43
Eulo 117, 140
Eurella 75, 139
Euthulla 75
Explosion of gas 83
F. B. Clapp and Co. 21
Ferguson, Sir George 28
Fire 100
Flinders River 29
Floods 33, 43, 71, 75, 77, 92, 109
Ford and Mylecharane 22
Forest Creek (Mount Alexander) 9
Fortitude Valley 28, 29
Francis, Sergeant 74
Franklin Vale 138
Fraser's Hotel, Toowoomba 131
Frazer's Creek 55
Freeman Cobb 9, 10, 21, 22, 25
Gallagher, Thomas 22
Gas 4, 7, 10, 12, 16, 43, 72, 73, 82, 83, 84, 85, 86, 88
Gas bore 82
Gas explosion 83
Gatton 30, 38, 39, 44, 138
Geelong 9, 10, 14, 21
George Francis Train 10, 25
George-street, Brisbane 29
Georgetown 10
Gippsland 21
Glenairn 56
Glengallen 43
Golden Fleece, Dalby 55
Goldfields 6, 9
Goondiwindi 138, 140
Gowrie Creek 43
Gowrie Junction 44, 141
Grafton 12, 71, 72, 83
Grafton Range 71, 72, 83
Great Dividing Range 43
Green Gate Hotel, Mitchell 57

Groom, William Henry 41
Guppy's Creek 56
Gympie 10, 28, 35, 118, 122
Handcock's store, Drayton 41
Harry H. Peck 10, 21
Haslin, John 109
Hay 22
Herberton 10
Hereford 11, 13
Hickson's butcher shop 43
Highfields 44
Hill and Fuller 9
Hiram Crawford 10
Hodgson 44, 71, 75, 88, 89, 90, 98, 136, 138, 141
Horton, William 41, 42, 134
Hotel Richards, Mitchell 57
Hughenden 110, 117
Humbug Creek 107
Hunt, Mr. 43
Hyland 9
Ipswich 10, 19, 22, 28, 30, 37, 41, 42, 44, 55, 76, 77, 90, 117, 131, 137, 138
Jack Howe 57
James Bevan and Co. 9
James Swanson 9, 22
James Watt 9
Jim Rutherford 11
John Lamber 9, 10, 21
John M. Peck 9
Johnson family 88, 89
John Wagner 10, 21
Jondaryan 43, 44, 55, 137, 138, 141
Juandah 55, 140
Kangaroo Point 28, 29, 30
Keegan, Thomas 88
Kitson Light Company 83
Kogan 55, 75, 109, 138
Kynuna 117
Lenroy 4, 7, 75, 88, 89, 90, 92, 93, 94, 95, 96, 97, 98
Limestone 41
Lister, J. 72
Llanheidol 117
lngledoon 11
London 11, 27, 29, 57, 74, 110
Long Creek 109
Longreach 82, 110, 117,

122
Lumber, Johnny 12
Lutwyche, Judge 28
Macalister 44, 71, 141
Mackay 11
Macquarie, Governor 27
Mail conveyance 7, 28, 55
Main Range 18, 41
Maitland 12, 42
Maranoa River 57, 108, 139
Marathon 117, 151
Margaret-street, Toowoomba 43
Martin, Mr. 77
Maryborough 10, 28, 89, 118, 137
Maryland 28, 55, 118, 137, 138, 140, 141
Maryvale 107, 138
McDowall-street, Roma 56, 71, 72
McPherson (Wild Scotchman) 75, 77
Mehan, David 41
Mehan, Stephen 41, 42
Meigs and Anderson 21
Melbourne 9, 10, 13, 21, 22, 108
Melbourne Omnibus Company 21
Miles 44, 56, 71, 72, 74, 117, 140, 141
Miranda Downs station 22
Mitchell 44, 56, 57, 68, 69, 71, 72, 88, 89, 108, 117, 132, 139, 140, 141
Mitchell Downs 57, 108
Moongool 57, 139
Moor Creek 107
Moore's Hotel, Roma 131
Moraby 108, 109
Moree 12
Moreton Bay 27, 28, 29, 41, 42, 142
Morgan, Godfrey 125
Morven 44, 90, 105, 117, 141
Motor buggies 7, 124, 125
Mount Abundance 71, 75, 99, 139
Mount Cootha/Mount Coottha 29
Muckadilla 44, 88, 105, 108, 141

Mugallala/Mungallala 44, 88, 141
Mungindi 12, 117, 141
Murrilla 55
Murrumbidgee Station 11
Murwillumbah 28
Myall 138
Myall Creek 55, 87, 138
Mylecharane and Elliott 9
Napoleon 27
National Museum, Canberra 126
Neila Ponds 117
Nerang 28, 29, 118
Nerang Creek 29, 118
New York State 11
New Zealand 12, 74, 83, 110
Nicholas, James 9
Nield, Guy 89
Nimmitabe 151
Nimmitabel 12
Noorindoo 56, 61, 140
Normanton 10
Northampton Downs 55
North Brisbane 29, 131
North Star Hotel, Ipswich 131
Nowland Bros. 9, 22
Nowlan's Royal Hotel, Brisbane 30
Oakey Creek 44, 141
Oberina, 77
Oil 82, 83, 84, 85, 86, 87, 88
One Tree Hill 29
Paddy's Creek 44, 141
Parkes 12
Paroo River 29
Parramatta 9, 43
Peak Hill 12
Peter Fleming and Co., Brisbane 30
Petrie's Bight, Brisbane 28
Pickenjenny 108
Poem - Cobb and Co. 106, 116, 124
Poem - Northward to the Shed 54
Poem - The Days of Cobb & Co. 132
Poem - The Drought-stricken Area 70
Poem - The Near-side Leader 8, 20, 26, 40
Point Lookout 27
Queen's Arms Hotel,

Roma 72, 74, 131
Queen's Arms Hotel, Toowoomba 74, 131
Queen's Arms, Roma 72
Queensborough 42
Queensland Hotel, Roma 74
Queensland Machinery Co. Ltd. 28
Queensland National Bank 29, 74
Queen-street, Brisbane 22, 28, 131
Railway 11, 12, 18, 19, 22, 29, 30, 36, 41, 42, 43, 44, 56, 57, 71, 72, 75, 76, 77, 107, 125, 126, 141
Railway Hotel, Roma 72
Rayner Family 89, 90, 98
Red Cow. Ipswich 42
Richmond 55, 117, 141
Richmond River Heads 55
Robberies 44, 77
Robertson, B. 21
Robertson, Britton and Co. 21
Robertson, C. 21
Rocky Bank 77, 141
Roma 4, 6, 7, 12, 19, 28, 29, 30, 44, 55, 56, 57, 67, 70, 71, 72, 73, 74, 75, 76, 77, 78, 79, 80, 81, 82, 83, 84, 85, 86, 87, 88, 89, 90, 91, 92, 93, 99, 100, 101, 102, 103, 104, 107, 108, 109, 110, 117, 118, 131, 138, 139, 140, 141
Roma Business Directory (1902) 74
Roma oil 82, 87
Roma residents (1902) 73
Roma-street, Brisbane 19
Roma Town Common 72
Roma Villa 90, 99
Royal Bull's Head Inn, Drayton 41, 42, 45
Royal Hotel, Dalby 109
Royal Hotel, Queen-street, Brisbane 30, 131
Royal Hotel, Roma 72
Royal Hotel, Wallumbilla 57
Royal Mail 57
Royal Mail Hotel, Wallumbulla 57
Russell-street, Toowoomba 41
Ruthven-street, Toowoomba 131
Ryland John Howard 9
Sandgate 22
Sandridge 10
San Francisco 12
Saw-mills 77
School of Arts Hotel, Roma 72
School of Arts, Roma 72
Scotland 27
Scott, Sir Walter 27
South Africa 12
South Brisbane 28, 29, 30, 131
Southport 6, 28
Sportsman's Arms Hotel, Miles 131
Spring Hill 28
Stamford 117
Stanthorpe 28, 118, 141
Stein's Bridge, Toowoomba 43
St George 56
Stirling's smithy 43
Stott's fellmongery 43
Stradbroke Island 27
Studdert, G. 22
Surat 4, 7, 55, 56, 57, 60, 61, 63, 67, 74, 77, 117, 125, 126, 127, 135, 138, 140, 141
Swanton, Blake, and Company 21
Sydney 9, 10, 11, 22, 27, 29, 56, 83, 90, 117, 125
Sydney Cove 27
Tallebudgera 28
Tambo 28, 110, 117, 140
Tara 125
Taree 12
Taroom 55, 77, 137, 138, 140, 141
Tattersall's Hotel, Ipswich 77
Tattersall's Hotel, Roma 74
Tchanning Creek 108, 139
Tenterfield 6, 11, 28, 55, 75, 88, 118, 140
Thallon 57, 117, 125
Thargomindah 117
The Big Rig 4, 7, 88, 90
The Royal Hotel, Hodgson 89
The Springs 41
The Swamp 9, 42
Thompson River 29
Tichborne, Jason 83
Timbarra Gold Diggings 55
Tolano tobacconist 72
Toowoomba 4, 6, 7, 12, 18, 29, 30, 40, 41, 42, 43, 44, 46, 47, 48, 49, 50, 51, 52, 53, 55, 71, 72, 73, 85, 110, 117, 130, 131, 137, 138, 141
Toowoomba Chronicle 42, 43, 44, 46
Townsville 29, 118
Traveller's Best Hotel 107
Trinidad 77, 140
Uhl's saddlery, Brisbane 28, 131
Undullah 55, 138, 140
Victoria 6, 9, 10, 11, 12, 14, 15, 16, 22, 25, 29, 34, 73, 74, 77, 107, 127, 131
Victoria Downs 107
Victorian Stage Company 21
Vinyards 99
Waldegrave 56, 63, 72, 74, 88, 136
Walker, Alexander 21
Wallann 55
Wallis, William 55
Wallumbilla 55, 57, 66, 76, 89, 108
Walter Hall 10, 21, 125
Wambo 55
Warenda 117
Warkon 55, 139, 140
Warra 44, 55, 137, 138, 141
Warra Warra 55, 138
Warrego district 22
Warrego River 107, 109
Warwick 6, 28, 29, 30, 41, 42, 43, 44, 55, 118, 130, 131, 137, 138, 141
Watson and Hewitt 21
Weather 57
Werribone 56
Werris Creek 12
Western Railway Hotel, Roma 74
Western Star Newspaper, Roma 72
Whitney, William Franklin 21
Wickham-street, Brisbane 83
Wilcannia 10, 22
Wilcannia road 22
Wines 43, 99
Winton 139
Witham, Captain 42, 131
Witham's Hotel, Toowoomba 42
Wodonga 10
Womallala 44, 141
Womba 109
Womballala 107, 108
Wombo 55, 137, 138
Wyagdon 11
Yalebone 77, 139
Yarra track 9
Yeulba 44, 56, 57, 63, 64, 65, 66, 71, 74, 75, 117, 125, 126, 127, 141
Younge's Royal Hotel, North Brisbane 131
Yowah station 22
Yuleba Creek 71